My Favourite
CRICKET STORIES

edited by
JOHN ARLOTT

To

ROBERT

with much affection

*First published in Great Britain in this collected form in
1974 by Lutterworth Press.*

*This edition published in 1986 by
Peerage Books
59 Grosvenor Street
London W1*

Introduction copyright © 1974 by John Arlott

*All the illustrations used in this book are the property of the editor,
Mr John Arlott, and reproduced by his kind permission, with the
exception of the Furniss drawings on page 11, which are reproduced
by kind permission of the Marylebone Cricket Club*

ISBN 1 85052 076 3

*Printed in Czechoslovakia
50631*

Contents

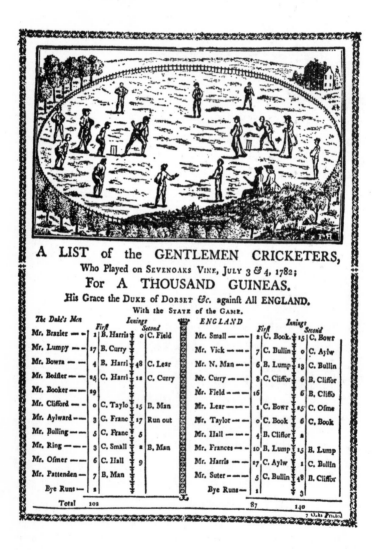

A LIST of the GENTLEMEN CRICKETERS,

Who Played on SEVENOAKS VINE, JULY 3 & 4, 1782;

For A THOUSAND GUINEAS.

His Grace the DUKE of DORSET &c. against All ENGLAND.

With the STATE of the GAME.

The Duke's Men	Innings First	Innings Second		ENGLAND	Innings First	Innings Second	
Mr. Brazier — —	1 B. Harris	0	C. Field	Mr. Small — — —	2 C. Book	15	C. Bowr
Mr. Lumpy — —	17 B. Curry			Mr. Vick — — —	7 C. Bullin	0	C. Aylw
Mr. Bowra — —	4 B. Harri	48	C. Lear	Mr. N. Man — —	6 B. Lump	13	C. Bullin
Mr. Bedfter — —	25 C. Harri	12	C. Curry	Mr. Curry — — —	8 C. Cliffor	6	B. Cliffor
Mr. Booker — —	29			Mr. Field — — —	16	6	B. Cliffo
Mr. Clifford — —	0 C. Taylo	15	B. Man	Mr. Lear — — —	1 C. Bowr	25	C. Ofme
Mr. Aylward — —	3 C. Franc	17	Run out	Mr. Taylor — —	0 C. Book	6	C. Book
Mr. Bulling — —	5 C. Franc	5		Mr. Hall — — —	4 B. Cliffor	2	
Mr. Ring — — —	3 C. Small	2	B. Man	Mr. Frances — —	10 B. Lump	15	B. Lump
Mr. Ofmer — —	6 C. Hall	9		Mr. Harris — —	27 C. Aylw	1	C. Bullin
Mr. Pattenden —	7 B. Man			Mr. Suter — —	5 C. Bullin	48	B. Cliffor
Bye Runs —	2			Bye Runs —	1	3	
Total	102				87	140	

7 Oaks Printed

Introduction

CRICKET HAS A WIDER literature than any other British sport. Yet, for all its extent, it is by no means always profound because of an unavoidable sameness. As an experienced fiction-writer once said, 'A sports story can only be about winning, losing or drawing.' So 'pure' cricket stories or accounts are limited in scope; and, unimaginatively handled, can be little more than exercises in arithmetic.

Cricket is, in essence, a contrived—though unpredictable —dramatic form. Its ingredients are runs, wickets and time, and those three factors in concert can produce high drama. They do not always combine to produce the thrilling finish; but when they do their effect can be extremely moving. On the whole, though, there tends to be a monotony about match accounts. The average reader knows the eventual result of most of the historic games and, without the element of suspense, the story is generally less than compelling.

The best cricket stories, however, do not depend on scores for their quality. They are concerned less with cricket than with cricketers. Indeed, they go far towards disproving the dictum that 'the game is greater than the players of the game'. They demonstrate that the character and personality of the performer are more absorbing than either the course or the outcome of play.

So, apart from Sir Neville Cardus's skilfully atmospheric evocation of the Oval Test match of 1882, Herbert Farjeon's gay legerdemain with the laws, and Sir Arthur Conan Doyle's nearly-possible fantasy, the stories in this book are about human beings, the essential material of any three-dimensional story.

For all Sir Neville's technical ability in reconstruction—and no one has done it better than he does in this example—his later piece on Tom Richardson is the more moving. A final look at the list shows that, quite unpremeditatedly, six of these pieces are fictional, and six fact.

The Story of Spedegue's Dropper must be the most neglected of all pieces of cricket fiction. Its author, Sir Arthur Conan Doyle, was a slow bowler and hard-hitting batsman who had some success in both capacities for M.C.C. sides against such opposition as Cambridgeshire and Leicestershire about 1900. He wrote an obituary appreciation of W. G. Grace for *The Times*, and it is said that Sherlock Holmes was named for the Nottinghamshire fast bowler, Frank Shacklock, and his brother Mycroft for the Derbyshire cricketing family of that name. Conan Doyle was a brother-in-law, friend and fellow cricket enthusiast of E. W. Hornung, whose character, 'Raffles, the amateur cracksman', was also a first-class slow left-arm bowler. In each of the Hornung stories, cricket is the setting—and an extremely authentic one—rather than the plot.

John Nyren's *Young Cricketer's Tutor* is the cricket classic, not for its main instructional section but for the later, nostalgic studies of his contemporaries, the Hampshire and Surrey village cricketers who are caught for ever in his sketches of *The Players of My Time*.

Ralph Barker's reconstruction of Harold Gimblett's remarkable first match century is a 'universal'; so is Mary Russell Mitford's country cricket match—a truly reflected facet of village life. Andrew Lang's Introduction for Richard Daft's *Kings of Cricket* was once described as the best essay ever written on the game: it holds the relationship between play and players in admirable perspective. R. C. Robertson-Glasgow—predictably christened 'Crusoe' early in his county career—the most perceptively witty of cricketer-writers, never thought the game greater than its players. Even at the height of his Test Match career, Arthur Mailey, cartoonist, painter, writer and leg spinner regarded cricket as a relishable, but not over-important, aspect of life. None of them thought the game too serious for humour.

6

The true test of any writing is that it appeals beyond the range of its subject; any cricketer should like a cricket story; but a good cricket story is not simply a cricketer's story—it is a story which will be appreciated by someone with no interest in the game. These pieces have been chosen with that criterion in mind.

John Arlott

January, 1974
Hampshire

I   *The Greatest Test Match*

SIR NEVILLE CARDUS

O N a bright day in the spring of 1921 I went to Lord's, hoping to see the first practice of the Australians. But the place was deserted, save for the man at the gates. He told me Armstrong's men were being entertained that afternoon somewhere in the City, and that they wouldn't be in the nets till after tea. Still, he added, with a touch of human nature not too common at Lord's, if I liked I could enter the ground and sit and enjoy myself in the sun till they came.

I sat on a bench with my feet spread out so that they touched the soft grass. A great calm was over the field. The trees beyond the 'nursery' were delicate with fresh green, and the fine old pavilion seemed to nod in the sunshine. It was an occasion for a reverie, and I fell to affectionate thoughts upon the great days of cricket, of the history that had been made on the field which stretched before me. I thought of Grace, of Spofforth, of Hornby, of A. G. Steel. . . . Maybe I dozed for a while. Then I was conscious of a voice. 'Would you mind moving up a little? This seat is rather congested.' I looked around and saw sitting by my side a man in a tight black coat which buttoned high on his chest. He had side whiskers and wore a low turned-down collar and a high bowler hat. A handkerchief was showing from a breast pocket in his jacket. Not quite awake yet, I 'moved up.' 'Thank you,' he said. 'I'm sorry I disturbed you. A nap carries one comfortably through a long wait at these matches. What a crowd there is!' I looked round. I was in the middle of a big crowd indeed. In front of me sat a parson. He was reading *The Times*. I glanced over his shoulder and saw the headline: 'Egyptian Campaign: Sir G. Wolseley's Despatch.' The man at my side said, 'Were you here yesterday, sir?' and before I could reply he added, 'It was a considerable day's cricket, and

9

the *Post* has an excellent account. Perhaps you've seen it?' He handed me a copy of the *Morning Post*, and, thanking him, I took it. The paper was dated August 29, 1882. In a column headed 'England v. Australia' I read that, on the day before, Australia had been dismissed for 63 by Barlow and Peate, and that England, captained by A. N. Hornby, had made in reply 101. Then I understood my situation. And what is more I now understood it without the slightest astonishment. Even the aspect of the ground, which told me it was Kennington Oval and not Lord's, did not embarrass me. It was enough that I was one of the crowd that was to witness the second day's cricket in the ninth Test match—the most famous Test match of all.

I gave the *Post* back to my companion in silence. 'A considerable day's cricket indeed, sir,' said the Parson. 'But England ought to have made more runs. Our batting was distinctly mediocre—almost as bad as the Australians'.' A loud cheer disturbed his argument. Down the pavilion steps walked the England Eleven in single file, led by Hornby. With him was W. G., and he passed along the field with an ambling motion, and the wind got into his great black beard. He spoke to Hornby in a high-pitched voice and laughed. Then he threw the ball to a tall, graceful player just behind him and cried, 'Catch her, Bunny.' Following Grace and Hornby were Lucas, C. T. Studd, J. M. Read, the Hon. A. Lyttelton, Ulyett, Barlow, W. Barnes, A. G. Steel and Peate. The crowd quietened, awaiting the advent of Australia's first two batsmen, and I again heard the Parson's voice's '. . . The English total was distressingly poor. Rarely have I seen poorer batting from an All England Eleven. The fact is, sir, that for some little time now English cricket has been deteriorating. Our batsmen don't hit the ball as hard as they used to do, and even our bowling . . .' Another cheer drowned his discourse. 'Bannerman and Massie,' said my companion. 'I should imagine Bannerman's the youngest man in the match.' The Parson was prompt with his correction. 'I believe S. P. Jones, who was twenty-one on the 1st of the month, is the junior member of the two teams.

A selection from the hundred drawings of Dr W. G. Grace contributed to *How's That* by the gifted caricaturist and illustrator, Harry Furniss (1854–1925). The originals of many of the drawings in this series are now at Lord's.

Reproduced by kind permission of the Marylebone Cricket Club

Studd, is, I fancy, eleven months older than Jones. Bannerman is twenty-three at least, and Giffen is six days younger than Bannerman.' My companion was silenced, but I ventured a question. 'How old is Spofforth?' Pat came the answer, 'Twenty-seven on the ninth of next month.'

The crowd, including even the Parson, went as quiet as a mouse as Barlow began the English bowling to Bannerman. Lyttelton, behind the wicket, crouched low. It was exactly a quarter past twelve. The next half-hour was a tumultuous prelude to the day. Bannerman was all vigilance, while Massie played one of the great innings of Test cricket. He hurled his bat at every ball the slightest loose, and his hits crashed ponderously to the boundary. He was the living image of defiance as he faced the Englishmen, glaring round the field his challenge. At one huge drive from Barlow's bowling my companion murmured, 'I've never seen a bigger hit than that at the Oval.' But the Parson overheard him. 'When the Australians were here in '78,' he said, 'W. H. Game, playing for Surrey, hit a ball from Spofforth to square leg right out of the ground.' Still, he admitted that this Massie fellow hit them quite hard enough. In half an hour England's advantage of 38 was gone. Hornby called up bowler after bowler, Studd for Barlow, Barnes for Studd. Steel tried his hand at 56—the sixth bowler in less than three-quarters of an hour. When Australia's score was 47 Massie lifted a ball to long on. 'Lucas is there,' said the Parson; 'he'll get it all r—Good Lord!' For Lucas dropped the ball and blushed red as the crowd groaned out of its soul.

'Sixty-six for none,' murmured the man at my side; 'they're 28 on with all their wickets intact. If Massie prevails—ah bravo, sir; well bowled, well bowled!' A ball from Steel had tempted Massie, and just as he jumped out it broke back and wrecked the wicket. Massie walked to the pavilion, roared home by an admiring but much relieved crowd. His innings was worth 55 to Australia, made out of 66 in less than an hour.

Bonnor came next, and the English out-fields dropped deep

and had apprehensive thoughts. Would not Massie's example make this bearded giant a very Jehu? But Hornby has an inspiration. He asks Ulyett to bowl instead of Steel. And Ulyett moves to the wicket like a man ploughing against a breaker, puts the last ounce of his Yorkshire strength into a thunderbolt of a ball that sends Bonnor's middle stump flying. The crowd is only just getting back the breath lost in approval of this feat when Bannerman is caught by Studd at extra mid-off. Bannerman has batted seventy minutes for 13. 'Quick work for him!' says the Parson. And with the broad bat of Bannerman out of the way the English bowlers begin to see daylight. Peate's slow left-hand deliveries spin beautifully, as though controlled by a string. The Australians now, save Murdoch, are just guessing. The fourth wicket falls at 75, the fifth at 79. Australia are all out 122. 'Only 85 to win,' says the Parson. 'It's our game after all, though Lucas did his best to lose it.'

It was a true autumn afternoon going to its fall in grey light when 'W.G.' and Hornby went to the wicket to face Spofforth and Garratt. The crowd filled the ground, but so silent was it as Grace took his guard that one could hear the tink-tink of a hansom cab coming closer and closer along the Vauxhall Road. Spofforth's first over was fast—he let the ball go with a quick leap, dropping his arm at the moment of release. Blackham 'stood back' when Grace was batting, but crept up for Hornby. 'Beautiful wicket-keeping,' murmured my companion. 'Pinder was not less gifted,' said the Parson. And he added, 'I have not seen Spofforth bowl as fast as this for some time. He has latterly cultivated medium-pace variations.' Both Hornby and Grace began confidently, and at once the tension lifted. Hornby made a lovely cut from Spofforth and a dainty leg stroke for a couple.

Spofforth uprooted Hornby's off stump with England's score 15, and with his next ball clean bowled Barlow. The crowd gave out a suspicion of a shiver, but the advent of bluff George Ulyett was reassuring, especially as Grace welcomed him with a fine leg hit from Garratt for three and a beautiful on drive to the boundary from Spofforth. 'Thirty up,' said my companion; 'only 55 to get.' England was still 30 for two when Spofforth crossed over to the pavilion end. Now I was behind his arm; I could see his superb break-back. And he bowled mainly medium-pace this time. With each off break I could see his right hand, at the end of the swing over, finish near the left side, 'cutting' under the ball. Sometimes his arm went straight over and continued straight down in the follow-through—and then the batsman had to tackle fierce top spin. There was the sense of the inimical in his aspect now. He seemed taller than he was a half-hour ago, the right arm of him more sinuous. There was no excitement in him; he was, the Parson said, cold-blooded. Still Ulyett faced him bravely while Grace, at the other end, time after time moved from his crease with a solid left leg and pushed the ball away usefully. 'Fifty up,' said my companion, 'for two wickets. It's all over—we want only 34 now.' And at 51 Spofforth bowled a very fast one to Ulyett, who barely snicked it. It served though; Blackham snapped the catch, and his 'Hzat!' was hoarse and aggressive. Lucas came in, and with two runs more 'W. G.' was caught at mid-off. 'What a stroke!' said the Parson. 'I'm afraid he's not the Grace he was.' Four for 53, and Lyttelton and Lucas in. Lyttelton hits out big-heartedly, but the field is like a net tightly drawn. It is suddenly understood by every man of us that the game is in the balance. 'The wicket must be bad,' says somebody.

Lucas stonewalls, with a bat as straight as a die. Spofforth bowls a maiden; Boyle bowls a maiden; Spofforth bowls another maiden. The air is growing thick. 'Get runs or get out, for the Lord's sake,' says somebody. The field creeps closer and closer to the wicket. Spofforth and Boyle are like uncanny automatons, bowling, bowling, bowling. . . . Six successive maidens. 'This,' says the Parson, 'this is intolerable.' One's heart is aching for an honest boundary hit. . . . And the human bowling machines send down six more successive maidens. Think of it; twelve successive maidens, and the game in that state, the crowd in that purgatory. 'When Grace was a boy of

14

eighteen I saw him make 50 on this very ground and he played every ball he got.' It was the Parson again, but now he sounded a little strained, a little unhappy. At the end of the twelfth successive maiden, a hit was purposely misfielded that Spofforth might have a 'go' at Lyttelton. The batsmen fell into the snare. Four more maidens, and spinning is Lyttelton's wicket. 'Anyhow, that's over and done with!' thankfully breathes the crowd. Better all be dead than dying! England five for 66—19 needed. Steel comes next and Lucas hits a boundary. Roars the crowd 'Bravo!' then catches breath. Steel caught and bowled Spofforth none—Maurice Read clean bowled second ball. England seven for 70. 'Incredible!' say 20,000 people in dismal unison. Barnes, the next man, hits a two. Thirteen to win. Heaven bless us, Blackham has blundered! He allows three byes. Run Barnes, run Lucas! Spofforth is inscrutable as the crowd makes its noises. His next ball is too fast for eyes at the boundary's edge to see. Lucas comes down on it, though —hard, determined. And the ball rolls ever so gently on to the wicket and disturbs the bail. Poor Lucas bows his head and departs, and blasphemy is riot throughout the crowd and is communicated by stages to the outer darkness of Kennington Road. The stars are set against England—our cricketers are for the first time on English soil face to face with a victorious Australian XI. With ten to struggle for, Blackham catches Barnes off his glove, and the last man is here—poor Peate, who is the best slow bowler in England and not a bit more of a cricketer than that, and what good are his mysteries of spin now? Studd is there yet, though; only ten runs and it is our game. Perhaps *he*—Peate has hit a two. It was audacious, but maybe the ball was a safe one to tackle. A bad ball's a bad ball at any time. Peate has nerve (so we are telling ourselves, desperately): the right man: he'll play the steady game to good stuff and leave the job to Studd. . . . The stark truth is that Peate hit out wildly yet again at a slow from Boyle, missed it, and was bowled. There was a hollow laugh somewhere as the wicket went back, but whether it came from this world or the next I couldn't say. Studd did not get a ball. 'Why, man, did you try to hit: why couldn't you just stop them?' they asked Peate. 'Well,' he replied, 'I couldn't trust Maister Studd!'

As Peate's wicket was broken, ten thousand people rushed the rails and hid the green field. Spofforth was carried shoulder-high to the pavilion, and there the mob praised a famous man. I, too, wanted to get up and shout, but somehow I was rooted to my seat. I was probably the only man in that multitude on the pavilion not standing up, and as I sat there I had a strange sense of making a lonely hole in a solid black mass. The Parson was standing on the seat beside me. His boots were not more than two feet from my eyes and I could see the fine ribbed work on the upper edge of the soles. The cheering came downwards to me, sounding remote. I lost grip on events. It seemed that I sat there till the ground was almost deserted, till over the field came a faint mist, and with it the vague melancholy of twilight in a great city. Time to go home, I thought . . . a great match . . . great days . . . great men . . . all gone . . . far away . . . departed glory. . . . A hand of someone touched my shoulder and I heard him say: 'The Orsetralians are on the way, and they'll be in the nets at four o'clock. Nice in the sun, isn't it?'

2   *Opposing My Hero*

ARTHUR MAILEY

MORE unemployment—and still I carried a cricket ball as I trudged the streets.

I had drifted into a lower grade of cricket, though it was still of fairly good standard, and I was told by some of my team-mates that I was capable of bowling a very dangerous ball. It didn't come up as often as it should, but it might lead to something. However, I should be well advised to lessen the spin and concentrate on length.

I was flattered that my fellow cricketers should think that even a few of the balls I delivered had devil in them. All the same, there was a rebellious imp sitting on my shoulder that whispered: 'Take no notice, cobber. They're crazy. Millions can bowl a good length but few can really spin the ball. Keep the spin and practise, practise, practise.'

Then came a commission for a house-painting job. It was a house near Botany Bay and it belonged to my brother-in-law. Wages? A bat that had been given to my brother-in-law by a distant relative who had taken part in the 1904 English tour. But what a relative! It was Victor Trumper himself—the fantastic, legendary Trumper, my particular hero. A hundred pounds could not have given me more pleasure.

Fancy getting a bat which my hero had actually used in a Test at Lord's: a flattish bat with a springy handle and a blade curved like the bowl of a spoon. This was another link closer to the great batsman and I was more than ever determined to improve my bowling.

The 'wrong 'un', that legacy from the great Bosanquet, like Bateman's 'one-note man' seemed to be getting me somewhere, for after several seasons in Sydney lower-grade teams I found

17

myself in first grade, a class of cricket in which inter-state and Test players participate.

At the same time, and having done my house-painting, I got another regular job. I became an A Class labourer on the Water and Sewage Board.

Things were certainly coming my way: I had never worn a collar and tie to work before. My mother had always hoped that I would get a 'white collar' job like Mr Rumble some day —and here it was.

It is difficult to realize that a relatively minor event in one's life can still remain the most important through the years. I was chosen to play for Redfern against Paddington—and Paddington was Victor Trumper's club.

This was unbelievable, fantastic. It could never happen— something was sure to go wrong. A war—an earthquake— Trumper might fall sick. A million things could crop up in the two or three days before the match.

I sat on my bed and looked at Trumper's picture still pinned on the canvas wall. It seemed to be breathing with the move- ment of the draught between the skirting. I glanced at his bat standing in a corner of the room, then back at the gently moving picture. I just couldn't believe that this, to me, ethereal and godlike figure could step off the wall, pick up the bat and say quietly, 'Two legs, please, umpire,' in my presence.

My family, usually undemonstrative and self-possessed, found it difficult to maintain that reserve which, strange as it may seem, was characteristic of my father's Northern Irish heritage.

'H'm,' said Father. 'Playing against Trumper on Saturday. By jove, you'll cop old harry if you're put on to bowl at him.'

'Why should he?' protested Mother. 'You never know what you can do till you try.'

I had nothing to say. I was little concerned with what should happen to me in the match. What worried me was that something would happen to Trumper which would prevent his playing.

Although at this time I had never seen Trumper play, on occasions I trudged from Waterloo across the Sandhills to the Sydney cricket ground and waited at the gate to watch the players coming out. Once I had climbed on a tram and actually sat opposite my hero for three stops. I would have gone further but having no money I did not want to take the chance of being kicked in the pants by the conductor. Even so I had been taken half a mile out of my way.

In my wildest dreams I never thought I would ever speak to Trumper let alone play against him. I am fairly phlegmatic by nature but between the period of my selection and the match I must have behaved like a half-wit.

Right up to my first Test match I always washed and pressed my own flannels, but before this match I pressed them not once but several times. On the Saturday I was up with the sparrows and looking anxiously at the sky. It was a lovely morning but it still might rain. Come to that, lots of things could happen in ten hours—there was still a chance that Vic could be taken ill or knocked down by a tram or twist his ankle or break his arm. . . .

My thoughts were interrupted by a vigorous thumping on the back gate. I looked out of the washhouse-bathroom-woodshed-workshop window and saw that it was the milkman who was kicking up the row.

'Hey!' he roared '—yer didn't leave the can out. I can't wait around here all day. A man should pour it in the garbage tin—that'd make yer wake up a bit!'

On that morning I wouldn't have cared whether he poured the milk in the garbage tin or all over me. I didn't belong to this world. I was playing against the great Victor Trumper. Let the milk take care of itself.

I kept looking at the clock. It might be slow—or it might have stopped! I'd better whip down to the Zetland Hotel and check up. Anyhow, I mightn't bowl at Trumper after all. He might get out before I come on. Or I mightn't get a bowl at all —after all, I can't put myself on. Wonder what Trumper's doing this very minute . . . bet he's not ironing his flannels. Sends them to the laundry, I suppose. He's probably got two sets of flannels anyway. Perhaps he's at breakfast, perhaps he's eating bacon and eggs. Wonder if he knows I'm playing against him? Don't suppose he's ever heard of me. Wouldn't worry him anyhow, I shouldn't think. Gosh, what a long morning! Think I'll dig the garden. No, I won't—I want to keep fresh. Think I'll lie down for a bit . . . better not, I might fall off to sleep and be late.

The morning did not pass in this way. Time just stopped. I couldn't bring myself to doing anything in particular and yet I couldn't settle to the thought of not doing anything. I was bowling to Trumper and I was not bowling to Trumper. I was early and I was late. In fact, I think I was slightly out of my mind.

I didn't get to the ground so very early after all, mainly because it would have been impossible for me to wait around so near the scene of Trumper's appearance—and yet for it to rain or news to come that something had prevented Vic from playing.

'Is he here?' I asked Harry Goddard, our captain, the moment I did arrive at the ground.

'Is who here?' he countered.

My answer was probably a scornful and disgusted look. I remember that it occurred to me to say, 'Julius Caesar, of course' but that I stopped myself being cheeky because this was one occasion when I couldn't afford to be.

Paddington won the toss and took first knock.

When Trumper walked out to bat, Harry Goddard said to me: 'I'd better keep you away from Vic. If he starts on you he'll probably knock you out of grade cricket.'

I was inclined to agree with him yet at the same time I didn't fear punishment from the master batsman. All I wanted to do was just to bowl at him. I suppose in their time other ambitious youngsters have wanted to play on the same stage with Henry Irving, or sing with Caruso or Melba, to fight with Napoleon or sail the seas with Columbus. It wasn't conquest I desired. I simply wanted to meet my hero on common ground.

Vic, beautifully clad in creamy, loose-fitting but well-tailored flannels, left the pavilion with his bat tucked under his left arm and in the act of donning his gloves. Although slightly pigeon-toed in the left foot he had a springy athletic walk and a tendency to shrug his shoulders every few minutes, a habit I understand he developed through trying to loosen his shirt off his shoulders when it became soaked with sweat during his innings.

Arriving at the wicket, he bent his bat handle almost to a right angle, walked up the pitch, prodded about six yards of it, returned to the batting crease and asked the umpire for 'two legs', took a quick glance in the direction of fine leg, shrugged his shoulders again and took up his stance.

I was called to bowl sooner than I had expected. I suspect now that Harry Goddard changed his mind and decided to put me out of my misery early in the piece.

Did I ever bowl that first ball? I don't remember. My head was in a whirl. I really think I fainted and the secret of the mythical first ball has been kept over all these years to save me embarrassment. If the ball *was* sent down it must have been hit for six, or at least four, because I was awakened from my trance by the thunderous booming Yabba who roared: 'O for a strong arm and a walking stick!'

I do remember the next ball. It was, I imagined, a perfect leg-break. When it left my hand it was singing sweetly like a humming top. The trajectory couldn't have been more graceful if designed by a professor of ballistics. The tremendous leg-spin caused the ball to swing and curve from the off and move in line with the middle and leg stump. Had I bowled this particular ball at any other batsman I would have turned my

21

back early in its flight and listened for the death rattle. However, consistent with my idolization of the champion, I watched his every movement.

He stood poised like a panther ready to spring. Down came his left foot to within a foot of the ball. The bat, swung from well over his shoulders, met the ball just as it fizzed off the pitch, and the next sound I heard was a rapping on the off-side fence.

It was the most beautiful shot I have ever seen.

The immortal Yabba made some attempt to say something but his voice faded away to the soft gurgle one hears at the end of a kookaburra's song. The only person on the ground who didn't watch the course of the ball was Victor Trumper. The moment he played it he turned his back, smacked down a few tufts of grass and prodded his way back to the batting crease. He knew where the ball was going.

What were my reactions?

Well, I never expected that ball or any other ball I could produce to get Trumper's wicket. But that being the best ball a bowler of my type could spin into being, I thought that at least Vic might have been forced to play a defensive shot, particularly as I was almost a stranger too and it might have been to his advantage to use discretion rather than valour.

After I had bowled one or two other reasonably good balls without success I found fresh hope in the thought that Trumper had found Bosanquet, creator of the 'wrong 'un' or 'bosie' (which I think a better name), rather puzzling. This left me with one shot in my locker, but if I didn't use it quickly I would be taken out of the firing line. I decided, therefore, to try this most undisciplined and cantankerous creation of the great B. J. Bosanquet—not, as many may think, as a compliment to the inventor but as the gallant farewell, so to speak, of a warrior who refused to surrender until all his ammunition was spent.

Again fortune was on my side in that I bowled the ball I had often dreamed of bowling. As with the leg-break, it had sufficient spin to curve in the air and break considerably after making contact with the pitch. If anything it might have had a little more top-spin, which would cause it to drop rather suddenly. The sensitivity of a spinning ball against a breeze is governed by the amount of spin imparted, and if a ball bowled at a certain pace drops on a certain spot, one bowled with identical pace but with more top-spin should drop eighteen inches or two feet shorter.

For this reason I thought the difference in the trajectory and ultimate landing of the ball might provide a measure of un-certainty in Trumper's mind. Whilst the ball was in flight this reasoning appeared to be vindicated by Trumper's initial movement. As at the beginning of my over he sprang in to attack but did not realize that the ball, being an off-break, was floating away from him and dropping a little quicker. Instead of his left foot being close to the ball it was a foot out of line.

In a split second Vic grasped this and tried to make up the deficiency with a wider swing of the bat. It was then I could see a passage-way to the stumps with our 'keeper, Con Hayes, ready to claim his victim. Vic's bat came through like a flash but the ball passed between his bat and legs, missed the leg stump by a fraction, and the bails were whipped off with the great batsman at least two yards out of his ground.

Vic had made no attempt to scramble back. He knew the ball had beaten him and was prepared to pay the penalty, and although he had little chance of regaining his crease on this occasion I think he would have acted similarly if his back foot had been only an inch from safety.

As he walked past me he smiled, patted the back of his bat and said, 'It was too good for me.'

There was no triumph in me as I watched the receding figure. I felt like a boy who had killed a dove.

3 *Introduction to* Kings of Cricket

ANDREW LANG

A CRICKETER is born, not made. A good eye and stout muscles are necessary; and though Mr Daft thinks highly of the intellectual element in cricket, it remains true that 'muscles make the man, not mind, nor that confounded intellect'.

Mr Daft has requested me to write an introduction to his *Kings of Cricket.* 'Anyone ought to make himself into a fair player by perseverance,' observes this authority. Alas! a long and bitter experience has taught me that there was one exception at least, to a rule which observation convinces me is far from general.

As to intellect, it is not so very hard to invent 'head balls'. After weeks of reflection, I once invented a 'head ball' myself. First, you send your man a ball tossed rather high, but really pitched rather short. The batsman detects this, or if he does not and goes in to drive it, so much the better. If he does detect it, you follow it up by a ball really pitched up, but of the same height in curve as the former. The batsman plays back again, thinking it is the same ball, and usually makes a mistake. Such studies in the subjectivity of the batsman are easily elaborated in the closet, but when it comes to practice he usually hits across the hop of the first ball and drives the second over the pavilion. In consequence of these failures to make the means attain the end, I have never taken part in really first-class cricket—not beyond playing once for my college eleven. But one beauty of cricket is that, if you cannot play at it, you can at least look on and talk very learnedly, and find fault with the captain, showing how you would order matters if you were consulted. This is the recreation of middle age, and is per-

25

mitted to an incapacity for actual performance which the audience never heard of or have had time to forget.

About Mr Daft's own play it is not possible, were it desirable, for me to offer criticism, as I never saw him save on one occasion. I had gone to Nottingham to view Gloucestershire play Notts, as two Clifton boys, friends of mine, were playing for the western county. One of them was bowling, and it is not ungracious to say that he was far from being a colossus. As Mr Daft came in, one of the crowd observed: 'I would like to see the little 'un bowl Daft!' which surely was a chivalrous expression of an Englishman's preference for the weaker side. However, the prayer was scattered to the winds. The ball, too, visited the boundaries of the Trent Bridge ground, and Notts made over five hundred.

Though one did not see very much first-class cricket before 1874, the memories of what one has seen and read about abide among our most pleasant reminiscences. Cricket is among the few institutions in England which Time has not spoiled, nay, has rather improved. The wickets are better, immeasurably better than of old. The bowling is better, the fielding is as good as ever; probably the wicket-keeping is improved, and the general temper of players and spectators leaves nothing to be desired. A fine day at the Oval makes us all akin, and a pleasant sight it is to see the vast assembly, every man with his eyes riveted on the wicket, every man able to appreciate the most delicate strokes in the game, and anxious to applaud friend or adversary. An English cricketing crowd is as fair and as generous as any assembly of mortals may be. When the Australians defeat us, though we do not like it, we applaud them till these bronzed Colonists almost blush. It is not so in all countries, nor in all countries is there the ready acceptance of the umpire's verdict, without which cricket degenerates into a wrangle.

Mr Daft is not inclined to believe that the veterans of a middle-aged man's youth were inferior to the heroes of our later day. With Dr W. G. Grace, indeed, no man competes or

26

has competed. The hardness and the subtlety of his hitting and placing of the ball, his reach and certainty at such a field as point, and the sagacious perseverance which he displays as a bowler, combine to make him unique—'W. G.,' a name to resound for ages.

There is somewhat monumental in his cricket wholly free from a false refinement, without extraneous elegancies. His is a nervous, sinewy, English style, like that of Fielding. Better graced cricketers we may have seen, such as Mr Edward Lyttelton, Mr Charles Studd, Mr A. G. Steel, all of them, in their day, models of classical dexterity and refinement. But it is always, or almost always, Dr W. G. Grace's day: his play is unhasting, unresting like the action of some great natural law. With him, then, nobody can compare; and we who have seen may report to the age unbred that ere they were born the flower of cricket had blossomed. Nevertheless, methinks that even before Fuller Pilch and Clarke, there had been very great cricketers, who, could they return in their prime, after a few weeks' practice might match our best.

Aylward, of Hampshire, must have been a truly sterling batsman. Lambert may also be reckoned among the immortals, and it is highly probable that David Harris, on those wickets which he knew how to prepare, would puzzle even men like Shrewsbury.

In these days the bowler laid out his wicket to suit himself. None of us now living can equal the old underhand bowling, which, in some mysterious way, was delivered high, from under the armpit, got up very fast and erect from the pitch, and was capable of many changes of curve and pitch. Brown, of Brighton, and others, appear to have bowled under-hand as fast, or faster, than Tarrant, or Jackson, or Mr Cecil Boyle.

This seems quite probable. Perhaps the swiftest bowling I ever saw was the underhand of a fast round-hand bowler, now in Canada, and at no time known to fame. He is a clergyman of the Scottish church, the 'Jointer,' so styled of yore. 'He says he's a meenister, he says he's a beginner; I think he's a leear,' observed the caddie, when asked, at golf, who this gentleman might be. Hail, Jointer, across the wide seas and the many years, I salute thee. *Bayéte!* as the Zulu says.

Now, allowing for odd wickets, and for the peculiarities of very fast underhand with a high delivery, it seems likely that, on an old Hampshire wicket, Nyren's team might have tackled as good an eleven as we moderns could send to meet them. In the fields of asphodel (which, of course, would need returfing), some such game may be played by heroes dead and gone.

But in this world one can never thus measure strength any more than we can judge of old actors, and compare Molière to Garrick, and Garrick to Monsieur Coquelin. The cricketer, un-like the actor, leaves something permanent—his scores; but we cannot discover the true equation, as the different conditions cannot be estimated. Thus in golf, a round of 94, on St Andrew's Links, in 1761, with feather balls, and unkempt putting greens, and whins all over the links, is surely, at least, as good as Hugh Kirkcaldy's round of 73 to-day, now that the iron age has come in, and the baffy spoon exists only as a venerable relic. Men's thews and skill have ever been much on a level.

It is the conditions that alter, and all old cricketers will believe in the old heroes of the past. To do so is pleasant, pious, and provides a creed not to be shaken by criticism. We who re-member Carpenter and Hayward, Caffyn and H. H. Stephen-son, are not to be divorced from these idols. They wore 'billy-cock' hats (the true word is 'bully-cock') and oddly-coloured shirts, and blue belts with snake clasps, and collars and neckties, as their great-grandfathers had worn jockey caps and knee-breeches, and their fathers tall hats. But these were unessential details.

The style in bowling of that age—Caffyn's age—with a level arm, was peculiarly graceful. The command of the ball was less than at present. Peate's delivery was level, or nearly level; yet his dexterity was unsurpassed. The most favourable ad-mirers can hardly call Mr Spofforth's style a model of grace. It has withal a something truculent and overbearing. Yet, on the modern wickets, bowling needs every fair advantage that it can obtain, and throwing has gone distinctly out of favour. I remember an excellent cricketer and most successful bowler, concerning whom I chanced to remark to a friend that I thought him quite fair. 'I think him a capital man to have on our side,' was the furthest to which my companion's lenity of judgment would stretch. Probably no bowler throws consciously, but it was certainly high time that umpires should bring some fast bowlers to the test of an objective standard. When round-hand bowling came in, the veteran Nyren declared that all was over with the game; that it would become a mere struggle of physical force. But, for this once, pessimism was mistaken, and prophecy was unfulfilled. Still there was the grace of a day that is dead in the old level deliveries, while some slinging bowlers, of whom Mr Powys, I think, was the last, could be extremely dangerous, if occasionally erratic. The regrets of him who praises times past are natural, but are tempered.

As for the present day, we are all tired—Mr Daft is tired—of the Fabian policy which leaves balls to the off alone, in a scientific cowardice. Once Mr Ernest Steel, then by no means a big boy, playing for Marlborough, at Lord's, taught a Rugby boy the unwisdom of this course. He bowled two balls to the off which were left alone; the third looked like them, but broke viciously, was let alone, and down went the off stump. This was not in first-class cricket, but it was a pleasant thing to see and remember. Many such pleasant memories recur to an old spectator.

There was Ulyett's catch, at Lord's, when the gigantic Mr Bonnor drove a ball to the off, invisible for its speed, and the public looked to see where the ring would divide. But the ball was in Ulyett's hands. There was Mr A. J. Webbe's catch of Mr Edward Lyttelton, who had hit a ball, low and swift as a half-topped golf ball, to the ropes. Running along the ropes, Mr Webbe caught it, low down, at full speed, a beautiful exhibition of graceful activity. Pinder would have commemorated it in an ode, and Dioscorides in a gem. Mr G. F. Grace's catch, under the pavilion at the Oval, I had not the fortune to witness, but Mr Gale has described it in impassioned prose.

Then there was Mr Steel's bowling, in his youthful prime, a sad sight for Oxford eyes, when the ball seemed alive and unplayable.

Mr Berkeley's bowling at Lord's, in 1891, at the end of the second Cambridge innings, was also a thing to dream upon, when for a moment it seemed as if the glories of Mr Cobden were to be repeated; but Mr Woods was there! As to Mr V. T. Hill's innings, in 1892, I cannot speak of it in prose.

Mr Daft has not dwelt much on University cricket, the most powerfully exciting to the spectator whose heart is in the right place (not unfrequently 'in his mouth') when we wait for a catch to come to hand.

The memories of old players in these affairs—Mr Mitchell, Mr Ottaway, Mr Yardley, Mr Steel, Mr Kemp (who won matches by sheer pluck and force of character), are fragrant and immortal. There is no talk, none so witty and brilliant, that is so good as cricket talk, when memory sharpens memory, and the dead live again—the regretted, the unforgotten—and the old happy days of burned out Junes revive. We shall not see them again. We lament that lost lightness of heart, 'for no man under the sun lives twice, outliving his day,' and the day of the cricketer is brief. It is not every one who can go on playing, 'once you come to forty years,' like Mr Daft and Dr W. G. Grace; the eye loses its quickness. An old man at point must be a very courageous old man; the hand loses its cunning, the ball from the veteran fingers has no work nor spin, and the idea of throwing in 'from the country' is painfully distasteful. Dr E. M. Grace, of course, is not old; he reckons not by years. Fortunately, golf exists as a solace of old age, and trout can always be angled for; and to lose a trout is only loss, not 'infinite dishonour,' like missing a catch.

Cricket is a very humanising game. It appeals to the emotions of local patriotism and pride. It is eminently unselfish; the love of it never leaves us, and binds all the brethren together, whatever their politics and rank may be. There is nothing like it in the sports of mankind. Everyone, however young, can try himself at it, though excellence be for the few, or perhaps not entirely for the few. At Nottingham, during the practice hour, how many wonderfully good bowlers you see, throwing off their coats and playing without even cricket shoes. How much good cricket there is in the world!

If a brief and desultory sermon may end with a collection, as is customary, I would fain ask cricketers to remember the London Playing Fields Committee, and send their mites to provide the grounds for those eager young players who draw their wickets with chalk on the wall, or bowl at a piled up heap of jackets. Their hearts are in the right place, if their wickets are not, and we can help to get them better grounds. Many good cricketers are on the Committee of the Playing Fields. I believe a cheque to Mr Theodore Hall, Oxford and Cambridge Club, Pall Mall, will go to the right place also. So pay up, that young town-bred boys may play up, ye merry men of England.

Cricket ought to be to English boys what Habeas Corpus is to Englishmen, as Mr Hughes says in *Tom Brown*.

At no ruinous expense, the village cricket might also be kept alive and improved; for cricket is a liberal education in itself, and demands temper and justice and perseverance. There is more teaching in the playground than in schoolrooms, and a lesson better worth learning very often. For there can be no good or enjoyable cricket without enthusiasm—without sentiment, one may almost say: a quality that enriches life and refines it; gives it, what life more and more is apt to lose, zest.

Though he who writes was ever a cricketing failure, he must acknowledge that no art has added so much to his pleasures as this English one, and that he has had happier hours at Lord's, or even on a rough country wicket, than at the Louvre or in the Uffizzi. If this be true of one, it is probably true of the

31

many whose pleasures are scant, and can seldom come from what is called culture.

Cricket is simply the most catholic and diffused, the most innocent, kindly, and manly of popular pleasures, while it has been the delight of statesmen and the relaxation of learning. There was an old Covenanting minister of the straitest sect, who had so high an opinion of curling that he said if he were to die in the afternoon, he could imagine no better way than curling of passing the morning. Surely we may say as much for cricket. Heaven (as the bishop said of the strawberry) might doubtless have devised a better diversion, but as certainly no better has been invented than that which grew up on the village greens of England.

4 *The Story of Spedegue's Dropper*

SIR ARTHUR CONAN DOYLE

THE name of Walter Scougall needs no introduction to the cricketing public. In the 'nineties he played for his University. Early in the century he began that long career in the county team which carried him up to the War. That great tragedy broke his heart for games, but he still served on his county Club Committee and was reckoned one of the best judges of the game in the United Kingdom.

Scougall, after his abandonment of active sport, was wont to take his exercise by long walks through the New Forest, upon the borders of which he was living. Like all wise men, he walked very silently through that wonderful waste, and in that way he was often privileged to see sights which are lost to the average heavy-stepping wayfarer. Once, late in the evening, it was a badger blundering towards its hole under a hollow bank. Often a little group of deer would be glimpsed in the open rides. Occasionally a fox would steal across the path and then dart off at the sight of the noiseless wayfarer. Then one day he saw a human sight which was more strange than any in the animal world.

In a narrow glade there stood two great oaks. They were thirty or forty feet apart, and the glade was spanned by a cord which connected them up. This cord was at least fifty feet above the ground, and it must have entailed no small effort to get it there. At each side of the cord a cricket stump had been placed at the usual distance from each other. A tall, thin young man in spectacles was lobbing balls, of which he seemed to have a good supply, from one end, while at the other end a lad of sixteen, wearing wicket-keeper's gloves, was catching those which missed the wicket. 'Catching' is the right word, for no ball struck the ground. Each was projected high up into the air and passed over the cord, descending at a very sharp angle on to the stumps.

Scougall stood for some minutes behind a holly bush watching this curious performance. At first it seemed pure lunacy, and then gradually he began to perceive a method in it. It was no easy matter to hurl a ball up over that cord and bring it down near the wicket. It needed a very correct trajectory. And yet this singular young man, using what the observer's practised eye recognized as a leg-break action which would entail a swerve in the air, lobbed up ball after ball either right on to the bails or into the wicket-keeper's hands just beyond them. Great practice was surely needed before he had attained such a degree of accuracy as this.

Finally his curiosity became so great that Scougall moved out into the glade, to the obvious surprise and embarrassment of the two performers. Had they been caught in some guilty action they could not have looked more unhappy. However, Scougall was a man of the world with a pleasant manner, and he soon put them at their ease.

'Excuse my butting in,' said he. 'I happened to be passing and I could not help being interested. I am an old cricketer, you see, and it appealed to me. Might I ask what you were trying to do?'

'Oh, I am just tossing up a few balls,' said the elder, modestly. 'You see, there is no decent ground about here, so my brother and I come out into the Forest.'

'Are you a bowler, then?'

'Well, of sorts.'

'What club do you play for?'

'It is only Wednesday and Saturday cricket. Bishops Bramley is our village.'

'But do you always bowl like that?'

'Oh, no. This is a new idea that I have been trying out.'

'Well, you seem to get it pretty accurately.'

'I am improving. I was all over the place at first. I didn't know what parish they would drop in. But now they are usually there or about it.'

'So I observe.'

'You said you were an old cricketer. May I ask your name?'

'Walter Scougall.'

The young man looked at him as a young pupil looks at the world-famed master.

'You remember the name, I see.'

'Walter Scougall. Oxford and Hampshire. Last played in 1913. Batting average for that season, twenty-seven point five. Bowling average, sixteen for seventy-two wickets.'

'Good Lord!'

The younger man, who had come across, burst out laughing.

'Tom is like that,' said he. 'He is Wisden and Lillywhite rolled into one. He could tell you anyone's record, and every county's record for this century.'

'Well, well! What a memory you must have!'

'Well, my heart is in the game,' said the young man, becoming amazingly confidential, as shy men will when they find a really sympathetic listener. 'But it's my heart that won't let me play it as I should wish to do. You see, I get asthma if I do too much—and palpitations. But they play me at Bishops Bramley for my slow bowling, and so long as I field slip I don't have too much running to do.'

'You say you have not tried these lobs, or whatever you may call them, in a match?'

'No, not yet. I want to get them perfect first. You see, it was my ambition to invent an entirely new ball. I am sure it can be done. Look at Bosanquet and the googlie. Just by using his brain he thought of and worked out the idea of concealed screw on the ball. I said to myself that Nature had handicapped me with a weak heart, but not with a weak brain, and that I might think out some new thing which was within the compass of my strength. Droppers, I call them. Spedegue's droppers—that's the name they may have some day.'

Scougall laughed. 'I don't want to discourage you, but I

wouldn't bank on it too much,' said he. 'A quick-eyed batsman would simply treat them as he would any other full toss and every ball would be a boundary.'

Spedegue's face fell. The words of Scougall were to him as the verdict of the High Court judge. Never had he spoken before with a first-class cricketer, and he had hardly the nerve to defend his own theory. It was the younger one who spoke.

'Perhaps, Mr Scougall, you have hardly thought it all out yet,' said he. 'Tom has given it a lot of consideration. You see, if the ball is tossed high enough it has a great pace as it falls. It's really like having a fast bowler from above. That's his idea. Then, of course, there's the field.'

'Ah, how would you place your field?'

'All on the on side bar one or two at the most,' cried Tom Spedegue, taking up the argument. 'I've nine to dispose of. I should have mid-off well up. That's all. Then I should have eight men to leg, three on the boundary, one mid-on, two square, one fine, and one a rover, so that the batsman would never quite know where he was. That's the idea.'

Scougall began to be serious. It was clear that this young fellow really had plotted the thing out. He walked across to the wicket.

'Chuck up one or two,' said he. 'Let me see how they look.' He brandished his walking-stick and waited expectant. The ball soared in the air and came down with unexpected speed just over the stump. Scougall looked more serious still. He had seen many cricket balls, but never quite from that angle, and it gave him food for thought.

'Have you ever tried it in public?'

'Never.'

'Don't you think it is about time?'

'Yes, I think I might.'

'When?'

'Well, I'm not generally on as a first bowler, I am second change as a rule. But if the skipper will let me have a go——'

'I'll see to that,' said Scougall. 'Do you play at Bishops Bramley?'

'Yes; it is our match of the year—against Mudford, you know.'

'Well, I think on Saturday I'd like to be there and see how it works.'

Sure enough Scougall turned up at the village match, to the great excitement of the two rural teams. He had a serious talk with the home captain, with the result that for the first time in his life Tom Spedegue was first bowler for his native village. What the other village thought of his remarkable droppers need not influence us much, since they would probably have been got out pretty cheaply by any sort of bowling. None the less, Scougall watched the procession to and from the cow-shed which served as a pavilion with an appreciative eye, and his views as to the possibilities lying in the dropper became clearer than before. At the end of the innings he touched the bowler upon the shoulder.

'That seems all right,' he said.

'No, I couldn't quite get the length—and, of course, they did drop catches.'

'Yes, I agree that you could do better. Now look here! you are second master at a school, are you not?'

'That is right.'

'You could get a day's leave if I wangled with the chief?'

'It might be done.'

'Well, I want you next Tuesday. Sir George Sanderson's house-party team is playing the Free Foresters at Ringwood. You must bowl for Sir George.'

Tom Spedegue flushed with pleasure.

'Oh, I say!' was all he could stammer out.

'I'll work it somehow or other. I suppose you don't bat?'

'Average nine,' said Spedegue, proudly.

Scougall laughed. 'Well, I noticed that you were not a bad fielder near the wicket.'

'I usually hold them.'

37

'Well, I'll see your boss, and you will hear from me again.'

Scougall was really taking a great deal of trouble in this small affair, for he went down to Totton and saw the rather grim head-master. It chanced, however, that the old man had been a bit of a sport in his day, and he relaxed when Scougall explained the inner meaning of it all. He laughed incredulously however, and shook his head when Scougall whispered some aspiration.

'Nonsense!' was his comment.

'Well, there is a chance.'

'Nonsense!' said the old man once again.

'It would be the making of your school.'

'It certainly would,' the head-master replied. 'But it is nonsense all the same.'

Scougall saw the head-master again on the morning after the Free Foresters match.

'You see it works all right,' he said.

'Yes, against third-class men.'

'Oh, I don't know. Donaldson was playing, and Murphy. They were not so bad. I tell you they are the most amazed set of men in Hampshire. I have bound them all over to silence.'

'Why?'

'Surprise is the essence of the matter. Now I'll take it a stage farther. By Jove, what a joke it would be!' The old cricketer and the sporting schoolmaster roared with laughter as they thought of the chances of the future.

All England was absorbed in one question at that moment. Politics, business, even taxation had passed from people's minds. The one engrossing subject was the fifth Test Match. Twice England had won by a narrow margin, and twice Australia had barely struggled to victory. Now in a week Lord's was to be the scene of the final and crucial battle of giants. What were the chances, and how was the English team to be made up?

It was an anxious time for the Selection Committee, and three more harassed men than Sir James Gilpin, Mr Tarding

and Dr Sloper were not to be found in London. They sat now
in the committee-room of the great pavilion, and they
moodily scanned the long list of possibles which lay before
them, weighing the claims of this man or that, closely inspect-
ing the latest returns from the county matches, and arguing
how far a good all-rounder was a better bargain than a man
who was supremely good in one department but weak in
another—such men, for example, as Worsley of Lancashire,
whose average was seventy-one, but who was a sluggard in the
field, or Scott of Leicestershire, who was near the top of the
bowling and quite at the foot of the batting averages. A week
of such work had turned the committee into three jaded old
men.

'There is the question of endurance,' said Sir James, the man
of many years and much experience. 'A three days' match is bad
enough, but this is to be played out and may last a week. Some
of these top average men are getting on in years.'

'Exactly,' said Tarding, who had himself captained England
again and again. 'I am all for young blood and new methods.
The trouble is that we know their bowling pretty well, and as
for them on a marled wicket they can play ours with their eyes
shut. Each side is likely to make five hundred per innings, and
a very little will make the difference between us and them.'

'It's just that very little that we have got to find,' said solemn
old Dr Sloper, who had the reputation of being the greatest
living authority upon the game. 'If we could give them something new! But, of course, they have played every county and
sampled everything we have got.'

'What can we ever have that is new?' cried Tarding. 'It is
all played out.'

'Well, I don't know,' said Sir James. 'Both the swerve and
the googlie have come along in our time. But Bosanquets
don't appear every day. We want brain as well as muscle
behind the ball.'

'Funny we should talk like this,' said Dr Sloper, taking a
letter from his pocket. 'This is from old Scougall, down in

Hampshire. He says he is at the end of a wire and is ready to come up if we want him. His whole argument is on the very lines we have been discussing. New blood, and a complete surprise—that is his slogan.'

'Does he suggest where we are to find it?'

'Well, as a matter of fact he does. He has dug up some un-known fellow from the back of beyond who plays for the second eleven of the Mudtown Blackbeetles or the Hinton Chawbacons or some such team, and he wants to put him straight in to play for England. Poor old Scougie has been out in the sun.'

'At the same time there is no better captain than Scougall used to be. I don't think we should put his opinion aside too easily. What does he say?'

'Well, he is simply red-hot about it. "A revelation to me." That is one phrase. "Could not have believed it if I had not seen it." "May find it out afterwards, but it is bound to upset them the first time." That is his view.'

'And where is the wonder man?'

'He has sent him up so that we can see him if we wish. Telephone the Thackeray Hotel, Bloomsbury.'

'Well, what do you say?'

'Oh, it's pure waste of time,' said Tarding. 'Such things don't happen, you know. Even if we approved of him, what would the country think and what would the Press say?'

Sir James stuck out his grizzled jaw. 'Damn the country and the Press, too!' said he. 'We are here to follow our own judgment, and I jolly well mean to do so.'

'Exactly,' said Dr Sloper.

Tarding shrugged his broad shoulders.

'We have enough to do without turning down a side-street like that,' said he. 'However, if you both think so, I won't stand in the way. Have him up by all means and let us see what we make of him.'

Half an hour later a very embarrassed young man was standing in front of the famous trio and listening to a series of very searching questions, to which he was giving such replies as he was able. Much of the ground which Scougall had covered in the Forest was explored by them once more.

'It boils down to this, Mr Spedegue. You've once in your life played in good company. That is the only criterion. What exactly did you do?'

Spedegue pulled a slip of paper, which was already frayed from much use, out of his waistcoat pocket.

'This is *The Hampshire Telegraph* account, sir.'

Sir James ran his eye over it and read snatches aloud. ' "Much amusement was caused by the bowling of Mr T. E. Spedegue." Hum! That's rather two-edged. Bowling should not be a comic turn. After all, cricket is a serious game. Seven wickets for thirty-four. Well, that's better. Donaldson is a good man. You got him, I see. And Murphy, too! Well, now, would you mind going into the pavilion and waiting? You will find some pictures there that will amuse you if you value the history of the game. We'll send for you presently.'

When the youth had gone the Selection Committee looked at each other in puzzled silence.

'You simply can't do it!' said Tarding at last. 'You can't face it. To play a bumpkin like that because he once got seven wickets for thirty-four in country-house cricket is sheer madness. I won't be a party to it.'

'Wait a bit, though! Wait a bit!' cried Sir James. 'Let us thresh it out a little before we decide.'

So they threshed it out, and in half an hour they sent for Tom Spedegue once more. Sir James sat with his elbows on the table and his finger-tips touching while he held forth in his best judicial manner. His conclusion was a remarkable one.

'So it comes to this, Mr Spedegue, that we all three want to be on surer ground before we take a step which would rightly expose us to the most tremendous public criticism. You will therefore remain in London, and at three-forty-five tomorrow morning, which is just after dawn, you will come down in your flannels to the side entrance of Lord's. We will, under pledge of secrecy, assemble twelve or thirteen groundmen whom we can trust, including half-a-dozen first-class bats. We will have a wicket prepared on the practice ground, and we will try you out under proper conditions with your ten fielders and all. If you fail, there is an end. If you make good, we may consider your claim.'

'Good gracious, sir, I made no claim.'

'Well, your friend Scougall did for you. But anyhow, that's how we have fixed it. We shall be there, of course, and a few others whose opinion we can trust. If you care to wire Scougall he can come too. But the whole thing is secret, for we quite see the point that it must be a complete surprise or a wash-out. So you will keep your mouth shut and we shall do the same.'

Thus it came about that one of the most curious games in the history of cricket was played on the Lord's ground next morning. There is a high wall round that part, but early wayfarers as they passed were amazed to hear the voices of the players, and the occasional crack of the ball at such an hour. The superstitious might almost have imagined that the spirits of the great departed were once again at work, and that the adventurous explorer might get a peep at the bushy black beard of the old giant or Billie Murdoch leading his Cornstalks once more to victory. At six o'clock the impromptu match was over, and the Selection Committee had taken the bravest and most sensational decision that had ever been hazarded since first a team was chosen. Tom Spedegue should play next week for England.

'Mind you,' said Tarding, 'if the beggar lets us down I simply won't face the music. I warn you of that. I'll have a taxi waiting at the gate and a passport in my pocket. Poste restante, Paris. That's me for the rest of the summer.'

'Cheer up, old chap,' said Sir James. 'Our conscience is clear. We have acted for the best. Dash it all, we have ten good men, anyhow. If the worst came to the worst, it only means one passenger in the team.'

'But it won't come to the worst,' said Dr Sloper, stoutly.

'Hang it, we have seen with our own eyes. What more can we do? All the same, for the first time in my life I'll have a whisky-and-soda before breakfast.'

Next day the list was published and the buzz began. Ten of the men might have been expected. These were Challen and Jones, as fast bowlers, and Widley, the slow left-hander. Then Peters, Moir, Jackson, Wilson, and Grieve were at the head of the batting averages, none of them under fifty, which was pretty good near the close of a wet season. Hanwell and Gordon were two all-rounders who were always sure of their places, dangerous bats, good change bowlers, and as active as cats in the field. So far so good. But who the Evil One was Thomas E. Spedegue? Never was there such a ferment in Fleet Street and such blank ignorance upon the part of 'our well-informed correspondent.' Special Commissioners darted here and there, questioning well-known cricketers, only to find that they were as much in the dark as themselves. Nobody knew—or if anyone did know, he was bound by oath not to tell. The wildest tales flew abroad. 'We are able to assure the public that Spedegue is a "nom de jeu" and conceals the identity of a world-famed cricketer who for family reasons is not permitted to reveal his true self.' 'Thomas E. Spedegue will surprise the crowd at Lord's by appearing as a coal-black gentleman from Jamaica. He came over with the last West Indian team, settled in Derbyshire, and is now eligible to play for England, though why he should be asked to do so is still a mystery.' 'Spedegue, as is now generally known, is a half-caste Malay who exhibited extraordinary cricket proficiency some years ago in Rangoon. It is said that he plays in a loin-cloth and can catch as well with his feet as with his hands. The question of whether he is qualified for England is a most debatable one.' 'Spedegue, Thomas E., is the headmaster of a famous northern school whose wonderful talents in the cricket field have been concealed by his devotion to his academic duties. Those who know him best are assured,' etc., etc. The Committee also began to get it in the neck. 'Why, with the wealth of talent available, these three elderly gentlemen, whose ideas of selection seem to be to pick names out of a bag, should choose one who, whatever his hidden virtues, is certainly un-used to first-class cricket, far less to Test Matches, is one of those things which make one realize that the lunacy laws are not sufficiently comprehensive.' These were fair samples of the comments.

And then the inevitable came to pass. When Fleet Street is out for something it invariably gets it. No one quite knows how *The Daily Sportsman* succeeded in getting at Thomas Spedegue, but it was a great scoop and the incredible secret was revealed. There was a leader and there was an interview with the village patriarch which set London roaring with laughter. 'No, we ain't surprised nohow,' said Gaffer Hobbs. 'Maister Spedegue do be turble clever with them slow balls of his'n. He sure was too much for them chaps what came in the char-a-bancs from Mudford. Artful, I call 'im. You'll see.' The leader was scathing. 'The Committee certainly seem to have taken leave of their senses. Perhaps there is time even now to alter their absurd decision. It is almost an insult to our Australian visitors. It is obvious that the true place for Mr Thomas Spedegue, however artful he may be, is the village green and not Lord's, and that his competence to deal with the char-a-bancers of Mudford is a small guarantee that he can play first-class cricket. The whole thing is a deplorable mistake, and it is time that pressure was put upon the Selection Board to make them reconsider their decision.'

'We have examined the score-book of the Bishops Bramley village club,' wrote another critic. 'It is kept in the tap-room of The Spotted Cow, and makes amusing reading. Our Test Match aspirant is hard to trace, as he played usually for the second eleven, and in any case there was no one capable of keeping an analysis. However, we must take such comfort as we can from his batting averages. This year he has actually amassed a hundred runs in nine recorded innings. Best in an innings, fifteen. Average, eleven. Last year he was less fortunate and came out with an average of nine. The youth is second master at the Totton High School and is in indifferent health, suffering from occasional attacks of asthma. And he is chosen to play for England! Is it a joke or what? We think that the public will hardly see the humour of it, nor will the Selection Committee find it a laughing matter if they persist in their preposterous action,' So spoke the Press, but there were, it is only fair to say, other journals which took a more charitable view. 'After all,' said the sporting correspondent of *The Times*, 'Sir James and his two colleagues are old and experienced players with a unique knowledge of the game. Since we have placed our affairs in their hands we must be content to leave them there. They have their own knowledge and their own private information of which we are ignorant. We can but trust them and await the event.'

As to the three, they refused in any way to compromise or to bend to the storm. They gave no explanations, made no excuses, and simply dug in and lay quiet. So the world waited till the day came round.

We all remember what glorious weather it was. The heat and the perfect Bulli-earth wicket, so far as England could supply that commodity, reminded our visitors of their native conditions. It was England, however, who got the best of that ironed shirt-front wicket, for in their first knock even Cotsmore, the Australian giant, who was said to be faster than Gregory and more wily than Spofforth, could seldom get the ball bail-high. He bowled with splendid vim and courage, but his analysis at the end of the day only showed three wickets for a hundred and forty-two. Storr, the googlie merchant, had a better showing with four for ninety-six. Cade's mediums accounted for two wickets, and Moir, the English captain, was run out. He had made seventy-three first, and Peters, Grieve, and Hanwell raked up sixty-four, fifty-seven, and fifty-one respectively, while nearly everyone was in double figures. The only exception was 'Thomas E. Spedegue, Esq.,' to quote the score card, which recorded a blank after his name. He was caught in the slips off the fast bowler, and, as he admitted afterwards that he had never for an instant seen the ball, and could hardly in his nervousness see the bowler, it is remarkable that his wicket was intact. The English total was four hundred and thirty-two, and the making of it consumed the whole of the first day. It was fast scoring in the time, and the crowd were fully satisfied with the result.

And now came the turn of Australia. An hour before play began forty thousand people had assembled, and by the time that the umpire came out the gates had to be closed, for there was not standing room within those classic precincts. Then came the English team, strolling out to the wickets and tossing the ball from hand to hand in time-honoured fashion. Finally appeared the two batsmen, Morland, the famous Victorian, the man of the quick feet and the supple wrists, whom many looked upon as the premier batsman of the world, and the stonewaller, Donahue, who had broken the hearts of so many bowlers with his obdurate defence. It was he who took the first over, which was delivered by Challen of Yorkshire, the raging, tearing fast bowler of the North. He sent down six beauties, but each of them came back to him down the pitch from that impenetrable half-cock shot which was characteristic of the famous Queenslander. It was a maiden over.

And now Moir tossed the ball to Spedegue and motioned him to begin at the pavilion end. The English captain had been present at the surreptitious trial and he had an idea of the general programme, but it took him some time and some consultation with the nervous, twitching bowler before he could set the field. When it was finally arranged the huge audience gasped with surprise and the batsmen gazed round them as if they could hardly believe their eyes. One poor little figure, alone upon a prairie, broke the solitude of the off-side. He stood as a deep point or as a silly mid-off. The on-side looked like a mass meeting. The fielders were in each other's way, and kept shuffling about to open up separate lines. It took some time to arrange, while Spedegue stood at the crease with a

46

nervous smile, fingering the ball and waiting for orders. The Selection Board were grouped in the open window of the committee-room, and their faces were drawn and haggard.

'My God! This is awful!' muttered Tarding.

'Got that cab?' asked Dr Sloper, with a ghastly smile.

'Got it! It is my one stand-by.'

'Room for three in it?' said Sir James. 'Gracious, he has got five short-legs and no slip. Well, well, get to it! Anything is better than waiting.'

There was a deadly hush as Spedegue delivered his first ball. It was an ordinary slow full pitch straight on the wicket. At any other time Morland would have slammed it to the boundary, but he was puzzled and cautious after all this mysterious setting of the field. Some unknown trap seemed to have been set for him. Therefore he played the ball quietly back to the bowler and set himself for the next one, which was similar and treated in the same way.

Spedegue had lost his nerve. He simply could not, before this vast multitude of critics, send up the grotesque ball which he had invented. Therefore he compromised, which was the most fatal of all courses. He lobbed up balls which were high but not high enough. They were simply ordinary over-pitched, full-toss deliveries such as a batsman sees when he has happy dreams and smiles in his sleep. Such was the third ball, which was a little to the off. Morland sent it like a bullet past the head of the lonely mid-off and it crashed against the distant rails. The three men in the window looked at each other and the sweat was on their brows. The next ball was again a juicy full toss on the level of the batsman's ribs. He banged it through the crowd of fielders on the on with a deft turn of the wrist which insured that it should be upon the ground. Then, gaining confidence, he waited for the next of those wonderful dream balls, and steadying himself for a mighty fast-footed swipe he knocked it clean over the ring and on to the roof of the hotel to square-leg. There were roars of applause, for a British crowd loves a lofty hit, whoever may deliver it. The scoreboard marked fourteen made off five balls. Such an opening to a Test Match had never been seen.

'We thought he might break a record, and by Jove he has!' said Tarding, bitterly. Sir James chewed his ragged moustache and Sloper twisted his fingers together in agony. Moir, who was fielding at mid-on, stepped across to the unhappy bowler.

'Chuck 'em up, as you did on Tuesday morning. Buck up, man! Don't funk it! You'll do them yet.'

Spedegue grasped the ball convulsively and nerved himself to send it high into the air. For a moment he pictured the New Forest glade, the white line of cord, and his young brother waiting behind the stump. But his nerve was gone, and with it his accuracy. There were roars of laughter as the ball went fifty feet into the air, which were redoubled when the wicket-keeper had to sprint back in order to catch it and the umpire stretched his arms out to signal a wide.

For the last ball, as he realized, that he was likely to bowl in the match, Spedegue approached the crease. The field was swimming round him. That yell of laughter which had greeted his effort had been the last straw. His nerve was broken. But there is a point when pure despair and desperation come to a man's aid—when he says to himself, 'Nothing matters now. All is lost. It can't be worse than it is. Therefore I may as well let myself go.' Never in all his practice had he bowled a ball as high as the one which now, to the amused delight of the crowd, went soaring into the air. Up it went and up—the most absurd ball ever delivered in a cricket match. The umpire broke down and shrieked with laughter, while even the amazed fielders joined in the general yell. The ball, after its huge parabola, descended well over the wicket, but as it was still within reach Morland, with a broad grin on his sun-burned face, turned round and tapped it past the wicket-keeper's ear to the boundary. Spedegue's face drooped towards the ground. The bitterness of death was on him. It was all over. He had let down the Committee, he had let down the side, he had let down England. He wished the ground would open and swallow him so that his only memorial should be a scar upon the pitch of Lord's.

And then suddenly the derisive laughter of the crowd was stilled, for it was seen that an incredible thing had happened. Morland was walking towards the pavilion. As he passed Spedegue he made a good-humoured flourish of his bat as if he would hit him over the head with it. At the same time the wicket-keeper stooped and picked something off the ground. It was a bail. Forgetful of his position and with all his thoughts upon this extraordinary ball which was soaring over his head, the great batsman had touched the wicket with his toe. Spedegue had a respite. The laughter was changing to applause. Moir came over and clapped him jovially upon the back. The scoring board showed total fifteen, last man fourteen, wickets one.

Challen sent down another over of fizzers to the impenetrable Donahue which resulted in a snick for two and a boundary off his legs. And then off the last ball a miracle occurred. Spedegue was fielding at fine slip, when he saw a red flash come towards him low on the right. He thrust out a clutching hand and there was the beautiful new ball right in the middle of his tingling palm. How it got there he had no idea, but what odds so long as the stonewaller would stonewall no more? Spedegue, from being the butt, was becoming the hero of the crowd. They cheered rapturously when he approached the crease for his second over. The board was twenty-one, six, two.

But now it was a very different Spedegue. His fears had fallen from him. His confidence had returned. If he did nothing more he had at least done his share. But he would do much more. It had all come back to him, his sense of distance, his delicacy of delivery, his appreciation of curves. He had found his length and he meant to keep it.

The splendid Australian batsmen, those active, clear-eyed men who could smile at our fast bowling and make the best of our slow bowlers seem simple, were absolutely at sea. Here was something of which they had never heard, for which they had never prepared, and which was unlike anything in the history of cricket. Spedegue had got his fifty-foot trajectory to a nicety, bowling over the wicket with a marked curve from the leg. Every ball fell on or near the top of the stumps. He was as accurate as a human howitzer pitching shells. Batten, who followed Morland, hit across one of them and was clean bowled. Staker tried to cut one off his wicket, and knocked down his own off-stump, broke his bat, and finally saw the ball descend amid the general *débris*. Here and there one was turned to leg and once a short one was hit out of the ground. The fast bowler sent the fifth batsman's leg-stump flying and the score was five for thirty-seven. Then in successive balls Spedegue got Bollard and Whitelaw, the one caught at the wicket and the other at short square-leg. There was a stand between Moon and Carter, who put on twenty runs between them with a succession of narrow escapes from the droppers. Then each of them became victims, one getting his body in front, and the other being splendidly caught by Hanwell on the ropes. The last man was run out and the innings closed for seventy-four.

The crowd had begun by cheering and laughing, but now they had got beyond it and sat in a sort of awed silence as people might who were contemplating a miracle. Half-way through the innings Tarding had leaned forward and had grasped the hand of each of his colleagues. Sir James leaned back in his deck-chair and lit a large cigar. Dr Sloper mopped his brow with his famous red handkerchief. 'It's all right, but, by George! I wouldn't go through it again,' he murmured. The effect upon the players themselves was curious. The English seemed apologetic, as though not sure themselves that such novel means could be justified. The Australians were dazed and a little resentful. 'What price quoits?' said Batten, the captain, as he passed into the pavilion. Spedegue's figures were seven wickets for thirty-one.

And now the question arose whether the miracle would be repeated. Once more Donahue and Morland were at the

wicket. As to the poor stonewaller, it was speedily apparent
that he was helpless. How can you stonewall a ball which drops
perpendicularly upon your bails? He held his bat flat before
it as it fell in order to guard his wicket, and it simply popped
up three feet into the air and was held by the wicketkeeper. One
for nothing. Batten and Staker both hit lustily to leg and each
was caught by the mass meeting who waited for them. Soon,
however, it became apparent that the new attack was not in-
vincible, and that a quick, adaptive batsman could find his
own methods. Morland again and again brought off what is
now called the back drive—a stroke unheard of before—when
he turned and tapped the ball over the wicket-keeper's head to
the boundary. Now that a crash helmet has been added to the
stumper's equipment he is safer than he used to be, but Grieve
has admitted that he was glad that he had a weekly paper with
an insurance coupon in his cricket bag that day. A fielder was
placed on the boundary in line with the stumps, and then the
versatile Morland proceeded to elaborate those fine tips to
slip and tips to fine leg which are admitted now to be the only
proper treatment of the dropper. At the same time Whitelaw
took a pace back so as to be level with his wicket and topped
the droppers down to the off so that Spedegue had to bring two
of his legs across and so disarrange his whole plan of campaign.
The pair put on ninety for the fifth wicket, and when Whitelaw
at last got out, bowled by Hanwell, the score stood at one
hundred and thirty.

But from then onwards the case was hopeless. It is all very
well for a quick-eyed, active genius like Morland to adapt
himself in a moment to a new game, but it is too much to ask
of the average first-class cricketer, who, of all men, is most
accustomed to routine methods. The slogging bumpkin from
the village green would have made a better job of Spedegue
than did these great cricketers, to whom the orthodox method
was the only way. Every rule learned, every experience en-
dured, had in a moment become useless. How could you play
with a straight bat at a ball that fell from the clouds? They did

their best—as well, probably, as the English team would have done in their place—but their best made a poor show upon a scoring card. Morland remained a great master to the end and carried out his bat for a superb seventy-seven. The second innings came to a close at six o'clock on the second day of the match, the score being one hundred and seventy-four. Spedegue eight for sixty-one. England had won by an innings and one hundred and eighty-four runs.

Well, it was a wonderful day and it came to a wonderful close. It is a matter of history how the crowd broke the ropes, how they flooded the field, and how Spedegue, protesting loudly, was carried shoulder-high into the pavilion. Then came the cheering and the speeches. The hero of the day had to appear again and again. When they were weary of cheering him they cheered for Bishops Bramley. Then the English captain had to make a speech. 'Rather stand up to Cotsmore bowling on a ploughed field,' said he. Then it was the turn of Batten the Australian. 'You've beat us at something,' he said ruefully; 'don't quite know yet what it is. It's not what we call cricket down under.' Then the Selection Board were called for and they had the heartiest and best deserved cheer of them all. Tarding told them about the waiting cab. 'It's waiting yet,' he said, 'but I think I can now dismiss it.'

Spedegue played no more cricket. His heart would not stand it. His doctor declared that this one match had been one too many and that he must stand out in the future. But for good or for bad—for bad, as many think—he has left his mark upon the game for ever. The English were more amused than exultant over their surprise victory. The Australian papers were at first inclined to be resentful, but then the absurdity that a man from the second eleven of an unknown club should win a Test Match began to soak into them, and finally Sydney and Melbourne had joined London in its appreciation of the greatest joke in the history of cricket.

5   *Herecombe* v *Therecombe*

HERBERT FARJEON

SHARP practice in our national game is probably a good deal more common than most Englishmen would care to admit. Although it is true that the other side is seldom openly accused of cheating, there can be hardly a pavilion in the country which has not at some time in its existence creaked with dark whispering against the impartiality of umpires from men who have been given out lbw, or against the honour of wicket-keepers from men who cannot bring themselves to believe that such a ball could possibly have hit the stumps. League cricket in particular produces complaints from batsmen who are convinced that they were not really so much bowled or caught or stumped as tricked out. Yet I question whether any match has ever been conducted in a more thoroughly unsportsmanlike manner than a certain officially 'friendly' match between the old-world villages of Herecombe and Therecombe. In the annals of the game it will, I imagine, stand for all time as the only match in which, although there was not a drop of rain, although play continued uninterrupted through the whole afternoon, and although both sides had a knock, only two balls were bowled. That, I feel sure, must be one of the most remarkable of all the records unchronicled in the pages of Wisden.

Herecombe and Therecombe were old antagonists. For some reason, as irrelevant as it is mysterious, there was no love lost between them. The feud, I believe, went deeper (if anything can) than cricket. But after the sensational tie in which a Herecombe batsman, backing up, was run out before the delivery of the ball, and a Therecombe batsman, politely rolling the ball back to the bowler, was successfully appealed against for 'handling', small wonder that each side vowed to win the next encounter by hook or crook. And small wonder, perhaps, that even the winning of the toss by Herecombe was viewed by Therecombe with deep suspicion.

The Herecombe captain elected to bat. Of course, he had no idea when he marched to the wicket to open the innings that it would be over in one ball. It was an astonishing ball, striking a flint—the ground was like that—and skidding at right angles to square leg.

The Herecombe captain slashed at it, missed it, was dumb-founded, and audibly ejaculated 'Well, I declare!' Everybody on the ground heard him, including the Therecombe captain. And the Therecombe captain was not slow to seize his opportunity.

'Come along, boys!' shouted the Therecombe captain, and made for the pavilion. His boys followed him. Nobody, with the exception of the Therecombe captain, knew quite what was happening. An explanation was demanded. The explanation was given.

'Didn't your captain say he declared?' asked the Therecombe captain. 'Very well, then. Us to bat, boys, and one run to win!'

A heated discussion ensued. Everybody called everybody else a dirty swindler. Threats were levelled, fists were shaken. The umpires read the Laws of Cricket through three times. In the end they decided that the Herecombe captain had in-escapably, if unintentionally, declared. The Herecombe team thereupon proposed to chuck it.

But suddenly the light of battle glinted in the eye of the Herecombe captain.

'All right,' he said to the Therecombe captain, 'we're game! You go in and win *if you can!*'

Then he led his men on to the field, handed the ball to little Smith, who had never bowled in a match in his life but who had once won a local Marathon race, and whispered a few words of command in his ear.

The Therecombe batsmen came out. The umpire called

'Play!' Little Smith began a long, zig-zag run up to the wicket.

But before little Smith reached the bowling-crease, a queer thing happened. He doubled back. Then, like a dog after its tail, he began running round in circles.

What, gasped the spectators, was up with little Smith? Had he gone stark, staring mad? There he was—turning and twisting—twisting and turning—darting this way and that—hopping, skipping, jumping—a most eccentric run, indeed—but never delivering the ball.

'Hi!' growled the Therecombe batsman, 'what's your bowler think he's doing?'

'Oh,' drawled the Herecombe captain, grinning, 'just playing out time, you know, playing out time. . . .'

So that was it! Another heated discussion now arose. Crowds congregated round the umpires, who read the Laws of Cricket all over again, while little Smith kept on running. But they could find nothing in the Laws of Cricket limiting the length of a bowler's run. Apparently a bowler could run all day before delivering the ball, and apparently he meant to.

Hour after hour little Smith kept up his capering—a noble effort—the batsman sternly refusing to leave the wicket lest he should be bowled in his absence. The fieldsmen lay down at full length on the ground. Spectators went away and then came back again, to find little Smith still running. Longer and longer grew his shadow as the sun travelled into the west. The clock on the old church tower chimed five, then six, then seven.

And now a new point of discussion arose. It had been agreed that at seven o'clock stumps should be drawn. But was it legal to draw stumps in the middle of a ball? The umpires got together again and, after much cogitation, decided that it would not be legal.

Then things became really exciting.

Little Smith shouted that if that was so, then dang him if he would deliver the ball till it was pitch dark. Still the batsman stood grimly on guard, determined if possible to make a winning swipe when the chance came at last. Again the spectators departed—this time for supper. Again they returned —this time under a harvest moon.

And there were the fieldsmen still lying on the grass, there was the batsman still standing at the wicket, and there was little Smith, still running.

At ten o'clock came the climax. It was dark. The moon had disappeared behind a cloud. Half a dozen of the fieldsmen had taken up positions beside the wicket-keeper behind the stumps to prevent an untimely bye. Little Smith let fly.

The Therecombe batsman screwed up his eyes to pierce the gloom. He struck. He missed.

'Match drawn!' shouted the Herecombe captain.

It was not quite the end. During his long vigil, the batsman had been doing a bit of thinking. He now protested that if stumps could not be drawn in the middle of a ball, neither could they be drawn in the middle of an over. The umpires started to consider the latest point. But while they were debating, the Herecombe captain put an end to doubt by appealing against the light—a rare thing indeed for a fielding side to do— the umpires allowed the appeal, and the game was over.

Whether the umpires were right in all their rulings may be open to question. I think they were. In any case, it must be conceded that they had some very knotty points to solve, and that on the whole they appear to have discharged their duties conscientiously.

6 *Harold Gimblett*

RALPH BARKER

THE fair-haired youth with the broad shoulders and the rustic gait who spent a fortnight practising with the Somerset team on the county ground at Taunton in May 1935 could surely only be a farmer, or a farmhand, or perhaps a farmer's son. Certainly he didn't look anything like a county cricketer. That, anyway, at the end of his fortnight's trial, was the verdict of the Somerset committee.

'I don't think you'll be upset if I tell you,' said the great John Daniell, 'that you're not quite the chap we're looking for.' This bronzed youth of medium height with the straight-brushed hair no doubt enjoyed his village cricket, but in a trial lasting ten days, in which he had mixed with the county players and joined with them in their pre-season practice, he had looked anything but a potential county cricketer. He might make a useful bowler, and he was certainly good in the field, but his batting had been awkward and ungainly and hopelessly raw.

An excess of zeal by the secretary of the Watchet club had placed the lad in the invidious position of being a county reject. Yet it seemed that this would do the boy no harm. It had been evident that he had no ambitions to be a county player and was not much interested in first-class cricket. He had been pushed into it against his will and had only agreed to come to please the Watchet secretary, the irrepressible Billy Penny. The lad's name was Harold Gimblett.

'You needn't be in a hurry to go,' said John Daniell kindly, 'you can stay on till the end of the week and help the groundsman. We'll pay you for that. It'll give you a few shillings in your pocket to go home with.' And on the Friday afternoon he gratefully collected 35 shillings* from the secretary's office and then went off to pack his gear.

Harold Gimblett was the youngest of three sons of Somerset farmer Percy Gimblett. Born on the farm at Bicknoller, about 7 miles south-east of Watchet, on the Somerset coast, and 15 miles north-west of Taunton, Gimblett had spent his life in the shadow of the Quantocks, apart from five years at school near Barnstaple. There, at West Buckland School, he had been the youngest boy ever to play for the first eleven. He had got into the team in 1928 at the age of 13½, and had captained it in his last year in 1931. During this time he had developed steadily as a schoolboy cricketer without doing anything outstanding, and the thought of making a living from cricket had not even remotely occurred to him, nor was it one of his schoolboy dreams.

Like many youths of school-leaving age he had no fixed ideas about his future, no burning ambitions or aspirations. But he thought he might like to be an electrical engineer. This was the time of the depression, when there were over two million unemployed, and it was a difficult time for school-leavers. Eventually a friend of Percy Gimblett's offered to give the boy a start in the wholesale grocery trade in London. Gimblett went into digs in Kenton and travelled daily to the warehouse in Eastcheap.

He kept up his cricket, playing for the London Devonians in London club cricket at Harrow. But he soon found that town life didn't suit him. He had spent too much of his life at farming, milking the cows, shearing the sheep, gathering in the crops, ever to accustom himself to office hours and office suits and rush-hour travelling. His father was a general farmer, in the days before specialization, and the diversified life of the farm offered infinite variety and incident, not to mention Somerset loam, the Quantocks, and the open sky. He yearned to get back to it, and after sticking it in the city for nine months he wrote to his father and asked if he might join him and make

* £1.75

his life at home as a farmer. His father agreed, and at the end of the summer of 1932 he left the wholesale grocery trade and returned happily to Bicknoller. London had been an experience and it had taught him to recognize what he wanted in life.

That summer he decided to join Watchet Cricket Club. It was, he thought, just about the best club in the area. Although it was 7 miles away, he cycled there every evening, and directly after lunch on match days. On Monday evenings he and his team-mates would cut and roll the wicket for the mid-week game on Wednesday. Tuesday was net practice, and more rolling of the wicket. Wednesday was a match-day. On Thursday evenings they cut and rolled Saturday's wicket and had some more practice, and on Friday evenings they got the ground and the wicket finally ready for Saturday's game. Starting work as he did at 6.30 in the morning, it was a pretty full day. By the time Sunday came—although there were still jobs to be done on the farm—he was glad of a day's rest.

This was the pattern of his life for the next three years. And all the time his cricket was developing. He got into the first team at Watchet, batting No. 6. And he was a great favourite with Billy Penny, the lively, rotund little tailor who lived for cricket and had been secretary of Watchet Cricket Club for over 40 years. 'How do you manage to spend so much time watching cricket?' someone once asked Penny. 'I never go to a game of cricket,' answered Penny, 'without selling a suit.'

Penny was the sort of man who could talk his way into or out of anything. He told a story about how he went to the first-ever Cup Final at Wembley in 1923—without a ticket. There were many gate-crashers that day, but few managed to bluff their way, as Penny did, into the Royal Box. Dressed in a mackintosh and bowler, he was taken for a detective accompanying the Royal party. And it was Penny who, in May 1935, as a member of the executive committee of the Somerset county club, talked his colleagues into giving the young Harold Gimblett a trial.

It was Friday 17th May when Gimblett packed his bag prior

to returning to Bicknoller. Everyone had been wonderfully kind to him and done their best to make him feel at home, and he had been sensible of the honour the Somerset players had done him in treating him as one of themselves. They had been away playing Surrey at the Oval on the Monday and Tuesday immediately after he arrived, but otherwise they had spent the whole time at Taunton, playing one game, from Saturday to Tuesday, against Northants. He had enjoyed meeting characters like Arthur Wellard, Bill Andrews, Frank and Jack Lee, Wally Luckes, and Horace Hazell, but much as he admired their cricket he had no wish to share their life.

These six men, in May 1935, represented the entire professional staff of the Somerset County Cricket Club. The brothers Lee opened the batting, Wellard and Andrews opened the bowling, Horace Hazell bowled the spinners, and Wally Luckes kept wicket. The rest of the side was made up of selected amateurs. R. A. Ingle was captain, and J. C. White, C. C. Case, H. D. Burrough and L. Hawkins had played in both matches so far and were usually available. Other amateurs who played occasionally were C. J. P. Barnwell and E. F. Longrigg, while several others were available in the holidays. But in May and June there were often no more than twelve or thirteen recognized county players available, and for the game beginning next day, Saturday 18th May at Frome, there were only eleven, the same team that had played at the Oval a fortnight ago and at Taunton earlier in the week.

Late on Friday afternoon it was learned that Hawkins, through injury, would be unable to play. So far as was known, none of the other amateurs was available. Had the game been at Taunton it would have been possible to leave final selection of the side until the Saturday morning, by which time all the alternatives could have been canvassed. But tomorrow's game was at Frome. It was essential to name the side and arrange details of travel and accommodation that night.

It suddenly occurred to the members of the Somerset committee who happened to be present that they did in fact already have eleven players available. Harold Gimblett had been born in Somerset. He could play for his county at any time. Would it be handicapping the side out of all reason to let him play just this once?

'Farmer' White, most experienced of the Somerset cricketers, didn't think so. In a way it would be killing two birds with one stone. 'Play this lad Gimblett,' he advised. 'It'll keep Billy Penny quiet for a bit, and at least he won't let us down in the field.'

So it was decided. The rejected trialist was to play in one game, as a stop-gap. It would make no difference to the committee's decision. He would never make any runs against bowlers like Stan Nichols, Laurie Eastman and Peter Smith, and he wouldn't get a bowl unless things were desperate. But his fielding got him in.

John Daniell sent for him. 'You're playing for Somerset tomorrow against Essex,' he said. 'The game's at Frome. Can you get there?' Gimblett had been travelling to and from Taunton by bus daily from Bicknoller—it was much cheaper than going into digs. 'I can get a bus into Bridgwater, Mr Daniell,' he said. 'I expect I can get another bus from there.'

'It sounds a bit of a journey,' said Daniell, 'I'll arrange for someone with a car to pick you up in Bridgwater. Good luck.' After some discussion with the other players it was arranged that Wally Luckes would pick him up in Bridgwater. It meant an early start for Gimblett, but he was used to that.

The first bus to Bridgwater passed the farm at 6.30. Gimblett was up at half-past five. After a quick breakfast he picked up his cricket bag, carefully packed the night before, and set off for the bus stop. It was a 3-mile walk along the lane, but by taking a short cut across the fields he could reduce this to about 2 miles. He allowed himself half an hour.

Part of the short cut took him over rough, uneven ground below the foothills of the Quantocks. His leather cricket bag was heavy, and he kept transferring it from one hand to the other. He wasn't making the progress he wanted to make, he had no watch and was unsure of the time. He began to sweat. It was three years since he had had to worry about catching buses and trains. He was still about 500 yards from the roadway when he saw the single-decker bus plunging along between the hedgerows. He started to run. He would never get to the bus-stop in time, and he began to wave and shout. The bus stopped briefly, then moved off. He heard the final gearchange into top, mocking his last shouts.

There wouldn't be another bus for two hours. He was supposed to meet Wally Luckes at nine o'clock. It took the best part of an hour to get to Bridgwater by bus, with many stops and starts along a winding road. He wouldn't be there until half past nine. Wally Luckes would never wait that long.

He heard the whine of a motor behind him and turned to see a lorry lumbering down the road. It was just possible that it might be going to Bridgwater. He stepped into the roadway and hailed the driver.

'Where are you going, lad?'

'I want to get to Bridgwater.'

'I turn off long before that. Did you miss the bus?'

'Yes.'

'Jump in—we might catch it up.'

Gimblett climbed in beside the lorry driver, lugging his cricket bag after him. The driver noticed the bag.

'Playing cricket?'

'Yes.'

'In Bridgwater?'

'No, Frome.'

'That's a long way. How are you getting there?'

'I've got someone picking me up in Bridgwater.'

'Who are you playing for?'

'Somerset.'

The lorry driver took a sideways glance at his passenger and then stared straight ahead. There were always madmen on the road, even at half past six in the morning. He was glad when he overtook the bus and was able to set his passenger down. You never knew what he might be carrying in that bag.

Frome is a small country town of about 10,000 inhabitants, roughly midway between Bristol and Salisbury. Its cricket ground, on the outskirts of the town, is no different from a hundred other small-town cricket grounds. A low wall separates the ground from the road, and the playing area is enclosed by a wooden railing, painted white, similar to the rails on a racecourse. The wicket is pitched parallel to the road. Backing on to the stone wall, hiding the wicket from the road, is the only stand, of corrugated iron construction, about 40 yards long and 30 feet high, containing tiered wooden benches and holding perhaps five to six hundred people. The only other buildings are the pavilion and pavilion annexe, situated in the corner just inside the ground, with a view of the wicket from long-leg, or deep extra cover. The pavilion is nothing more than a low wooden shed, built on to the original corrugated iron shed, dignified here as the annexe. The playing area is small, perhaps 120 yards across and 100 yards long, and the square and straight boundaries are no more than 60 yards from the wicket. Cows graze on slightly rising ground just across the far leg boundary, and behind the screen to the left the ground slopes gently downhill, giving a pleasing view of the outskirts of Frome. To anyone accustomed to watching county cricket in a large provincial town, it is quite unrecognizable as a county ground.

But this is to miss the whole atmosphere of county cricket in the West Country. Come to this ground during the Frome Week and you will find it transformed. The grass area at the pavilion end of the ground will be *en fête* with marquees. Benches will be sited three deep outside the white railings, and a chair hire company will have covered the area round the screen at the pavilion end. This enclosing of the ground by Somerset folk will give it a shape and a unity which is not quite apparent for the rest of the year. The atmosphere will correspond to that of an agricultural show, where friends meet to discuss the merits of the cricketers instead of the cattle. Their talk of the cricketers is as intimate as of their families. You will not hear the names of Wellard and Andrews, or Luckes, or the Lees, mentioned at all. It will be Arthur and Bill, and Wally, and Frank and Jack. All their idiosyncrasies will be known and loved, all their tricks will be looked for, all their antics will meet with a ready response. The crowd is amongst the game and the players, far more than it can ever be at the Oval, or Edgbaston, or Old Trafford. There is no privacy for the players, and amongst their own people they neither want it nor need it. They rub shoulders with all.

Even so, the young Harold Gimblett, meeting people who for years had been no more than names to him—Jack O'Connor, Tom Pearce, Ray and Peter Smith, Stan Nichols, Laurie Eastman, and the umpires, Alfred Dipper and Frank Chester— was completely overawed. He didn't think at all about his innings—he didn't expect to get one. He was bound to be No. 11. But Ingle had had a word with two or three of his professionals and they had readily agreed that the new lad should be given every chance. He walked across to Gimblett.

'No. 8, Harold.'

'Yes, Mr Ingle.'

Wally Luckes and Bill Andrews, both good players, would be behind him at 9 and 10, with Horace Hazell No. 11.

It was a bitterly cold May morning, with a high wind blowing almost straight down the ground, but over a thousand people were there at the start and most of the benches were occupied. Somerset won the toss and elected to bat on a good, hard wicket. The brothers Lee opened to the bowling of Nichols, from the far end, with the wind behind him, and Ray Smith. The innings started badly. In fifty minutes Jack Lee, Ingle and White were all caught at slip off Nichols, and that was 35 for three. Then Frank Lee and C. C. Case put on 66 in an hour before Nichols, coming back to bowl the last three overs downwind before lunch, had Lee l.b.w. for 41. At the other end, Case hit Peter Smith for 4 and was then clean bowled by a googly last ball before lunch. After putting up the hundred with only three wickets down, Somerset were 105 for five and the innings was falling apart.

Only one more wicket had to fall and then Gimblett would be in. But although he was still silent and overawed, he felt no trace of nerves. To him it was just another game of cricket. So far as he was concerned he had nothing to lose, neither did he have anything to gain. He was quietly enjoying himself. He had had nothing to eat since his hurried breakfast nearly eight hours earlier, and he tucked in to a good lunch.

When the game restarted at 2.15, Arthur Wellard joined H. D. Burrough. Both were not out 0. One over accounted for Burrough. He took 2 off the fifth ball from Nichols and was then bowled by the last ball of the over.

No one in the crowd had heard of Gimblett and the bare name on the scorecard, shorn of initials, meant less than nothing. But his youthful appearance appealed to the crowd and they gave him a good reception. He left the pavilion enclosure with a barrage of advice echoing in his ears.

'Try to stay there while Arthur gets after them,' said Ingle.

'Watch Peter Smith,' said Wally Luckes, 'he's bound to bowl you a googly first ball.'

Gimblett had never encountered a googly, either during his season with the London Devonians or at Watchet, and he had only the vaguest idea what it was. But he knew it came in from the off.

'And don't forget you can be leg-before to a ball pitching outside the off stump now,' added Luckes, 'under the new rule.' The new experimental l.b.w. law had only just been introduced and was not yet in force outside first-class cricket.

It was twenty-past two when Gimblett got to the wicket. Somerset were 107 for six. Wellard, facing Peter Smith, took a single off the first ball, and Gimblett moved down to the far end, away from the pavilion. He took guard, then settled down into his upright stance. (Arthur Wellard, who had winced when he saw the bound, discoloured willow that Gimblett had intended to play with, had lent him a bat.) Too diffident to step back and survey the placing of the field, Gimblett prepared to face the first ball.

Peter Smith came up to bowl. The ball pitched outside the off stump and came in towards the wicket. He guessed it must be the googly. He made no flourishing defensive shot, but simply put his bat in the way. The next ball pitched outside the leg stump and spun across the wicket, and again he blocked it. The third ball was the googly again, and he detected it this time, stepping back and planting it firmly to mid-wicket. They went through for one run. At least he hadn't made a duck.

Now he was batting at the pavilion end, facing Nichols. The wind had dropped and the sun had come out, but he had never faced anyone half as fast as Nichols. The ball thundered down at tremendous pace, seeming to gather speed off the wicket. But he was young, and his reactions were quick. Another single came to him off Nichols's third ball.

Next over Peter Smith tossed one up to him and he swung his bat at it, just as though he were playing for Watchet. The ball flashed past Smith for 4. Then he took a single. In the pavilion the Somerset professionals shook their heads. He would never get away with this. 'Why doesn't he leave it to Arthur?' they demanded. Then they relaxed as Wellard took a single off the fifth ball. 'That's better. Arthur's kept the bowling.'

Wellard struck Nichols for two fours, and another 8 runs came in Peter Smith's next over, 7 of them to Gimblett, including another straight drive for 4. They had now made a dozen each and both looked surprisingly comfortable.

It was in Peter Smith's next over from the pavilion end, his fourth since lunch, that Gimblett really asserted himself, though he was not conscious of any such intention. Wellard took a single off the first ball, and Gimblett pulled the second for 4. He played defensively to the third, but the fourth, a leg-break, was pitched well up on the off stump and he swung at it with the full flow of the bat, aiming high over mid-off's head. He felt the ball on the middle of the bat and looked up to see it soaring over bowler and mid-off. When at last the trajectory curved earthwards the ball was far beyond the boundary. It landed with a plop on the top of the beer tent.

He had hit his first six. The crowd, anxious for him up to now, cheered excitedly and settled down to relish the cricket. Peter Smith still kept the ball up to him and he thumped the next one past him for 4. A single off the last ball brought him 15 runs off the over, taking his score to 35 and making the partnership worth 50. By strong, audacious forward play that could not be described as hitting, he was outscoring Arthur Wellard, the biggest and most consistent hitter in the game. Most of his shots were aimed in a comparatively narrow arc from widish mid-off to widish mid-on, but within this area they were struck with such power and variety that they were beating the field every time.

Exhortations to 'leave it to Arthur' were forgotten. 'He never batted like this in the nets,' said Jack White. This was echoed on all sides. The truth was that Gimblett felt caged and restricted at net practice and never looked anything like the player there that he did in the middle.

Another over each from Nichols and Peter Smith and they had bowled ten overs between them since lunch in well under half an hour. In this time 71 runs had been added for the loss of Burrough's wicket. Burrough had received the first over, and then in nine overs from two of the best bowlers in county cricket Gimblett and Wellard had added 69, of which Gimblett had made 48 and Wellard 21.

Tom Pearce, anxious to give Stan Nichols a rest before the new ball was due at 200, put on Vic Evans, a slow off-break bowler, at the end opposite the pavilion. Wellard tried to hit his second ball out of the ground but missed and was stumped by Wade. 176 for seven, if not a complete transformation, certainly put Somerset back in the game.

Luckes came in and took a single off Evans to keep the bowling. Pearce persisted with Peter Smith for the new batsman, but a leg-bye gave Gimblett the strike and the next ball, short of a length, he pulled far up the mound beyond the crowd at square leg for 6. Fortunately the farmer had moved his cows to another field. With this shot Gimblett reached his 50. He had been batting 28 minutes and had received only 33 balls.

Now Gimblett faced the slows of Vic Evans for the first time. He straight drove the first ball for 4, and took a single off the second. Pearce had two men deep behind the bowler but on this small ground they could not cut off Gimblett's full-blooded hits. A two and a one came from the first two balls of Peter Smith's next over, and Gimblett was now scoring off practically every ball. Nine runs off the next over from Evans, including two more boundaries, took his score to 72 and put up the 200. Pearce at once took the new ball.

A refreshed Nichols came on to bowl with the wind again from the Frome end. Having shown what he could do with top-class spin, Gimblett now attacked the new ball. He hit Nichols for a four and a three, then took a single off the first ball from Ray Smith. Luckes played out the over. Gimblett then late cut Nichols for his twelfth four, and a single off the fourth ball of the over took his score to 86. Two balls later Nichols at last got the new ball past the bat and clean bowled Luckes. Of the 47 put on for the eighth wicket in 23 minutes Luckes had made 7.

Again Gimblett took a single off Ray Smith's first ball, cutting him down to third man, and Andrews, the new batsman, scored 6 runs off the rest of the over. Now Nichols bowled his best over of the innings to Gimblett, giving him everything in his seam repertoire, and Gimblett, after scoring off almost every ball bowled to him in the previous half-hour, could not get a single ball away. It was the first maiden bowled to Gimblett in county cricket. At the other end Andrews got a single off Ray Smith's first ball and Gimblett cut the next one for 4, taking his score to 91. But the last four balls were right on a length, moving in the air and off the seam, and although he still played his shots at them he could not get the ball away.

Again Andrews contrived a single off the first ball of the over to give Gimblett the bowling, and this time Nichols pitched the ball further up and Gimblett drove him to the ring. For the last ball of this over Nichols tried a bouncer and Gimblett hooked him to the pavilion for another four to take his score to 99.

Only a handful of people near the pavilion knew that Gimblett was so close to his century. The scoreboard was of the crudest kind, showing nothing more than the total runs, the number of wickets down, and the score of the last man. Much frantic signalling went on between the overs as people round the tiny score-box tried to impart to the batsmen the vital information that Gimblett wanted only one for his hundred. It was no use. The word passed quickly round the ground but did not reach the wicket. Gimblett was aware of a commotion, but he had no idea that he was so near a century. Amidst mounting tension, Andrews played out the whole of Ray Smith's next over, leaving Gimblett to face Nichols for the last coveted run.

Nichols ran up to bowl, a splendid, powerful figure with a magnificent action. The ball was fast and true, right on the wicket, right on a length. Gimblett moved his left leg quickly forward and a moment later the bat came through, striking the ball firmly into the covers. The field was spread wide and it was an easy two.

Even if he never made another run in his life, the name of Harold Gimblett was now a part of cricket history. He had made a century on his first appearance in first-class cricket. Playing his natural game, just as he might have played at Watchet, without any wild hitting, he had made it in the astonishing time of 63 minutes. He had received 71 balls— about 12 overs—and he had made his 101 out of 130 scored while he was at the wicket. For much of the time his partners had been Wellard and Andrews—two of the biggest hitters in the game.

Somehow he failed to score off the next ball from Stan Nichols. But the third ball of the over was of a fairly full length. That free, effortless Gimblett swing, which was to give more pleasure to spectators than perhaps any other front-of-the-wicket shot after Hammond, was set in motion. The ball rose straight as a gun barrel, landing far beyond the screen for 6, rolling on down the slope towards Frome. Nichols glared down the wicket at him, then grinned. 'That *was* a good shot,' he conceded.

When Gimblett eventually gave a return catch to Laurie Eastman—he remembers even now his annoyance at making the shot—he had made 123 in 79 minutes and hit three sixes and seventeen fours. Less than 24 hours earlier he had been packing his bag to return home after failing his trial. Four days later he was playing against Middlesex at Lord's.

Somerset were all out by four o'clock for 337. After being 107 for six at one stage they proceeded to beat Essex by an innings. Essex had lost their grip on the game during Gimblett's innings and they never recovered it.

The question that everyone asked—including Gimblett—was, had it been a flash in the pan? Could he repeat it? When Gimblett made fifty at Lord's in his second game, he and Somerset decided that he could. He made only one other score of over fifty that season, and averaged only 18, but Somerset persevered with him, and day by day in the county game he began to learn how to bat. He did so well in 1936, his second season, that he played in two Test Matches against India and was a strong candidate for the Australian tour. But to the great regret of the Australians he never went there, not even after the war. He had a splendid season in 1946 and a good one in 1950, and it is a matter for the saddest reflection that he missed selection on both occasions. He was invited to play in the Third Test at Nottingham in 1950, when Ramadhin and Valentine

SOMERSET v ESSEX
Frome: May 18, 20 and 21, 1935

SOMERSET

J. W. Lee	c Pearce b Nichols ...	3
F. S. Lee	lbw Nichols	41
R. A. Ingle	c Eastman b Nichols ..	12
J. C. White	c Eastman b Nichols ..	4
C. C. Case	b Smith (P.)	35
H. D. Burrough	b Nichols	2
A. W. Wellard	st Wade b Evans	21
H. Gimblett	c and b Eastman	123
W. T. Luckes	b Nichols	7
W. H. R. Andrews	c O'Connor b Evans .	71
H. L. Hazell	not out	7
B 5, l-b 5, w 1		11
		337

ESSEX

J. A. Cutmore	lbw Wellard	24	b Lee (J.)	26
F. Rist	c Lee (J.) b. Wellard ..	41	c Wellard b Hazell ...	21
T. N. Pearce	b Wellard	1	st Luckes b Hazell ...	0
J. O'Connor	not out	30	c Burrough b Wellard .	25
M. S. Nichols	c Lee (J.) b Wellard ..	0	st Luckes b White	31
T. P. Lawrence	b Wellard	4	b Lee (J.)	6
L. C. Eastman	b Lee (J.)	35	lbw White	1
P. Smith	b Lee (J.)	0	c Ingle b Lee (J.)	22
T. H. Wade	c Wellard b Hazell ...	1	lbw Lee (J.)	9
V. J. Evans	c Wellard b Lee (J.) ..	2	st Luckes b Lee (J.)	1
R. Smith	lbw Lee (J.)	0	not out	0
L-b 2, n-b 1		3	B 2, l-b 3	5
		141		**147**

ESSEX......	O.	M.	R.	W.	O.	M.	R.	W.
Nichols......	23	3	87	·6				
Smith (R.)...	13	2	43	0				
Eastman.....	13	4	38	1				
Evans	14·5	1	69	2				
Smith (P.) ...	13	1	89	1				
SOMERSET								
Wellard	23	6	66	5	9	2	18	1
Andrews ...	7	1	20	0	1	0	5	0
White.......	16	8	16	0	15	4	31	2
Lee (J.)	10	1	26	4	21·5	5	67	5
Hazell	11	8	10	1	10	4	21	2

FALL OF WICKETS

	S.	Essex	S.	Essex
Wkt.	1st.	1st.	2nd	2nd
1st	11	52	41	
2nd	27	67	65	
3rd	35	70	65	
4th	101	74	102	
5th	105	82	110	
6th	107	131	114	
7th	176	131	114	
8th	223	135	132	
9th	282	141	133	

Somerset won by an innings and 49 runs.

were mesmerizing English batsmen—he had played a great innings against them for Somerset two months earlier—but he was suffering from a carbuncle on the back of the neck at the time and had to decline. He was then 35. He seems never to have been considered again, and he never went on a major overseas tour. We may indeed ask ourselves in retrospect how this could possibly be.

For many years Harold Gimblett enjoyed no more than moderate support from the other regular batsmen in the Somerset side, and there can be little doubt that in such circumstances runs are harder to get. Yet season after season he continued to play his natural game, untroubled by responsibility, regularly enjoying a high place in the English averages, and a higher place still amongst lovers of cricket. In those early post-war years no cricketer, not even Denis Compton, gave more pleasure than Harold Gimblett. His best season was 1952, when he set up what was then a new Somerset record with an aggregate of 2068 runs. It was a tragedy that after this exceptionally good season, and when still only 38, he was forced to retire through ill-health.

Like Compton again, Gimblett was a cricketing genius, accountable to no one, absolutely unique. In thirteen seasons, from 1935 to 1939 and from 1946 to 1953, he scored 22,966 runs for an average of 36.23, and he hit 50 centuries including that storybook innings at Frome.

7   *Gentlemen and Players*

E. W. HORNUNG

OLD Raffles may or may not have been an exceptional criminal, but as a cricketer I dare swear he was unique. Himself a dangerous bat, a brilliant field, and perhaps the very finest slow bowler of his decade, he took incredibly little interest in the game at large. He never went up to Lord's without his cricket-bag, or showed the slightest interest in the result of a match in which he was not himself engaged. Nor was this mere hateful egotism on his part. He professed to have lost all enthusiasm for the game, and to keep it up only for the very lowest motives.

'Cricket,' said Raffles, 'like everything else, is good enough sport until you discover a better. As a source of excitement it isn't in it with other things you wot of, Bunny, and the involuntary comparison becomes a bore. What's the satisfaction of taking a man's wicket when you want his spoons? Still, if you can bowl a bit your low cunning won't get rusty, and always looking for the weak spot's just the kind of mental exercise one wants. Yes, perhaps there's some affinity between the two things after all. But I'd chuck up cricket tomorrow, Bunny, if it wasn't for the glorious protection it affords a person of my proclivities.'

'How so?' said I. 'It brings you before the public, I should have thought, far more than is either safe or wise.'

'My dear Bunny, that's exactly where you make a mistake. To follow crime with reasonable impunity you simply must have a parallel ostensible career—the more public the better. The principle is obvious. Mr Peace, of pious memory, disarmed suspicion by acquiring a local reputation for playing the fiddle and taming animals, and it's my profound conviction that Jack the Ripper was a really eminent public man, whose speeches were very likely reported alongside his atrocities. Fill the bill in some prominent part, and you'll never be suspected of doubling it with another of equal prominence. That's why I want you to cultivate journalism, my boy, and sign all you can. And it's the one and only reason why I don't burn my bats for firewood.'

Nevertheless, when he did play there was no keener performer on the field, nor one more anxious to do well for his side. I remember how he went to the nets, before the first match of the season, with his pocket full of sovereigns, which he put on the stumps instead of bails. It was a sight to see the professionals bowling like demons for the hard cash, for whenever a stump was hit a pound was tossed to the bowler and another balanced in its stead, while one man took £3 with a ball that spread-eagled the wicket. Raffles's practice cost him either eight or nine sovereigns; but he had absolutely first-class bowling all the time, and he made fifty-seven runs next day.

It became my pleasure to accompany him to all his matches, to watch every ball he bowled, or played, or fielded, and to sit chatting with him in the pavilion when he was doing none of these three things. You might have seen us there, side by side, during the greater part of the Gentlemen's first innings against the Players (who had lost the toss) on the second Monday in July. We were to be seen, but not heard, for Raffles had failed to score, and was uncommonly cross for a player who cared so little for the game. Merely taciturn with me, he was positively rude to more than one member who wanted to know how it had happened, or who ventured to commiserate with him on his luck; there he sat, with a straw hat tilted over his nose and a cigarette stuck between lips that curled disagreeably at every advance. I was, therefore, much surprised when a young fellow of the exquisite type came and squeezed himself in between us, and met with a perfectly civil reception despite the liberty. I did not know the boy by sight, nor did Raffles introduce us; but their conversation proclaimed at once a slightness of acquaintanceship and a licence on the lad's part which combined to puzzle me. Mystification reached its height when Raffles was informed that the other's father was anxious to meet him, and he instantly consented to gratify that whim.

'He's in the Ladies' Enclosure. Will you come round now?'

'With pleasure,' says Raffles.—'Keep a place for me, Bunny.'

And they were gone.

'Young Crowley,' said some voice further back. 'Last year's Harrow Eleven.'

'I remember him. Worst man in the team.'

'Keen cricketer, however. Stopped till he was twenty to get his colours. Governor made him. Keen breed. Oh, pretty, sir! Very pretty!'

The game was boring me. I only came to see old Raffles perform. Soon I was looking wistfully for his return, and at length I saw him beckoning me from the palings to the right.

'Want to introduce you to old Amersteth,' he whispered, when I joined him. 'They've a cricket week next month, when this boy Crowley comes of age, and we've both got to go down and play.'

'Both!' I echoed. 'But I'm no cricketer!'

'Shut up,' says Raffles. 'Leave that to me. I've been lying for all I'm worth,' he added sepulchrally, as we reached the bottom of the steps. 'I trust to you not to give the show away.'

There was the gleam in his eye that I knew well enough elsewhere, but was unprepared for in those healthy, sane surroundings; and it was with very definite misgivings and surmises that I followed the Zingari blazer through the vast flower-bed of hats and bonnets that bloomed beneath the ladies' awning.

Lord Amersteth was a fine-looking man with a short moustache and a double chin. He received me with much dry courtesy, through which, however, it was not difficult to read a less flattering tale. I was accepted as the inevitable appendage of the invaluable Raffles, with whom I felt deeply incensed as I made my bow.

75

'I have been bold enough,' said Lord Amersteth, 'to ask one of the Gentlemen of England to come down and play some rustic cricket for us next month. He is kind enough to say that he would have liked nothing better, but for this little fishing expedition of yours, Mr——, Mr——,' and Lord Amersteth succeeded in remembering my name.

It was, of course, the first I had ever heard of that fishing expedition, but I made haste to say that it could easily, and should certainly, be put off. Raffles gleamed approval through his eyelashes. Lord Amersteth bowed and shrugged.

'You're very good, I'm sure,' said he. 'But I understand you're a cricketer yourself?'

'He was one at school,' said Raffles, with infamous readiness.

'Not a real cricketer,' I was stammering meanwhile.

'In the eleven?' said Lord Amersteth.

'I'm afraid not,' said I.

'But only just out of it,' declared Raffles, to my horror.

'Well, well, we can't all play for the Gentlemen,' said Lord Amersteth slyly. 'My son Crowley only just scraped into the eleven at Harrow, and he's going to play. I may even come in myself at a pinch; so you won't be the only duffer, if you are one, and I shall be very glad if you will come down and help us too. You shall flog a stream before breakfast and after dinner, if you like.'

'I should be very proud,' I was beginning, as the mere prelude to resolute excuses; but the eye of Raffles opened wide upon me; and I hesitated weakly, to be duly lost.

'Then that's settled,' said Lord Amersteth, with the slightest suspicion of grimness. 'It's to be a little week, you know, when my son comes of age. We play the Free Foresters, the Dorsetshire Gentlemen, and probably some local lot as well. But Mr Raffles will tell you all about it, and Crowley shall write.— Another wicket! By jove, they're all out! Then I rely on you both.' And, with a little nod, Lord Amersteth rose and sidled into the gangway.

76

Raffles rose also, but I caught the sleeve of his blazer.

'What are you thinking of?' I whispered savagely. 'I was nowhere near the eleven. I'm no sort of cricketer. I shall have to get out of this!'

'Not you,' he whispered back. 'You needn't play, but come you must. If you wait for me after half-past six I'll tell you why.'

But I could guess the reason; and I am ashamed to say that it revolted me much less than did the notion of making a public fool of myself on a cricket-field. My gorge rose at this as it no longer rose at crime, and it was in no tranquil humour that I strolled about the ground while Raffles disappeared in the pavilion. Nor was my annoyance lessened by a little meeting I witnessed between young Crowley and his father, who shrugged as he stopped and stooped to convey some information which made the young man look a little blank. It may have been pure self-consciousness on my part, but I could have sworn that the trouble was their inability to secure the great Raffles without his insignificant friend.

Then the bell rang, and I climbed to the top of the pavilion to watch Raffles bowl. No subtleties are lost up there; and if ever a bowler was full of them, it was A. J. Raffles on this day, as, indeed, all the cricket world remembers. One had not to be a cricketer oneself to appreciate his perfect command of pitch and break, his beautifully easy action, which never varied with the varying pace, his great ball on the leg-stump—his dropping head-ball—in a word, the infinite ingenuity of that versatile attack. It was no mere exhibition of athletic prowess, it was an intellectual treat, and one with a special significance in my eyes. I saw the 'affinity between the two things,' saw it in that afternoon's tireless warfare against the flower of professional cricket. It was not that Raffles took many wickets for few runs; he was too fine a bowler to mind being hit; and time was short, and the wicket good. What I admired, and what I remember, was the combination of resource and cunning, of patience and precision, of head-work and handiwork, which made every over an artistic whole. It was all so characteristic of that other Raffles whom I alone knew!

'I felt like bowling this afternoon,' he told me later—in the hansom. 'With a pitch to help me, I'd have done something big; as it is, three for forty-one, out of the four that fell, isn't so bad for a slow bowler on a plumb wicket against those fellows. But I felt venomous! Nothing riles me more than being asked about for my cricket as though I were a pro. myself.'

'Then why on earth go?'

'To punish them, and—because we shall be jolly hard up, Bunny, before the season's over!'

'Ah!' said I. 'I thought it was that.'

'Of course it was! It seems they're going to have the very devil of a week of it—balls—dinner-parties—swagger house-party—general junketings—and obviously a houseful of diamonds as well. Diamonds galore! As a general rule nothing would induce me to abuse my position as a guest. I've never done it, Bunny. But in this case we're engaged like the waiters and the band, and by heaven we'll take our toll! Let's have a quiet dinner somewhere and talk it over.'

'It seems rather a vulgar sort of theft,' I could not help saying; and to this, my single protest, Raffles instantly assented.

'It is a vulgar sort,' said he; 'but I can't help that. We're getting vulgarly hard up again, and there's an end on't. Besides,

78

these people deserve it, and can afford it. And don't you run away with the idea that all will be plain sailing; nothing will be easier than getting some stuff, and nothing harder than avoiding all suspicion, as, of course, we must. We may come away with no more than a good working plan of the premises. Who knows? In any case there's weeks of thinking in it for you and me.'

But with those weeks I will not weary you further than by remarking that the 'thinking' was done entirely by Raffles, who did not always trouble to communicate his thoughts to me. His reticence, however, was no longer an irritant. I began to accept

it as a necessary convention of these little enterprises. And, after our last adventure of the kind, more especially after its *dénoue-ment*, my trust in Raffles was much too solid to be shaken by a want of trust in me, which I still believe to have been more the instinct of the criminal than the judgment of the man.

It was on Monday, August 10, that we were due at Milchester Abbey, Dorset; and the beginning of the month found us cruising about that very county, with fly-rods actually in our hands. The idea was that we should acquire at once a local reputation as decent fishermen, and some knowledge of the country-side, with a view to further and more deliberate operations in the event of an unprofitable week. There was another idea which Raffles kept to himself until he had got me down there. Then one day he produced a cricket-ball in a meadow we were crossing, and threw me catches for an hour together. More hours he spent in bowling to me on the nearest green; and, if I was never a cricketer, at least I came nearer to being one by the end of that week than ever before or since.

Incident began early on the Monday. We had sallied forth from a desolate little junction within quite a few miles of Milchester, had been caught in a shower, had run for shelter to a wayside inn. A florid, over-dressed man was drinking in the parlour, and I could have sworn it was at the sight of him that Raffles recoiled on the threshold, and afterwards insisted on returning to the station through the rain. He assured me, however, that the odour of stale ale had almost knocked him down. And I had to make what I could of his speculative, downcast eyes and knitted brows.

Milchester Abbey is a grey, quadrangular pile, deep-set in rich woody country, and twinkling with triple rows of quaint windows, every one of which seemed alight as we drove up just in time to dress for dinner. The carriage had whirled us under I know not how many triumphal arches in process of construction, and past the tents and flag-poles of a juicy-looking cricket-field, on which Raffles undertook to bowl up to his reputation. But the chief signs of festival were within, where we found an enormous house-party assembled, including more persons of pomp, majesty, and dominion than I had ever encountered in one room before. I confess I felt over-powered. Our errand and my own pretences combined to rob me of an address upon which I had sometimes plumed myself; and I have a grim recollection of my nervous relief when dinner was at last announced. I little knew what an ordeal it was to prove.

I had taken in a much less formidable young lady than might have fallen to my lot. Indeed I began by blessing my good fortune in this respect. Miss Melhuish was merely the rector's daughter, and she had only been asked to make an even number.

She informed me of both facts before the soup reached us, and
her subsequent conversation was characterised by the same en-
gaging candour. It exposed what was little short of a mania
for imparting information. I had simply to listen, to nod, and
to be thankful. When I confessed to knowing very few of those
present, even by sight, my entertaining companion proceeded
to tell me who everybody was, beginning on my left and
working conscientiously round to her right. This lasted quite a
long time, and really interested me; but a great deal that
followed did not; and, obviously to recapture my unworthy
attention, Miss Melhuish suddenly asked me, in a sensational
whisper, whether I could keep a secret.

I said I thought I might, whereupon another question
followed, in still lower and more thrilling accents:

'Are you afraid of burglars?'

Burglars! I was roused at last. The word stabbed me. I
repeated it in a horrified query.

'So I've found something to interest you at last!' said Miss
Melhuish, in naive triumph. 'Yes—burglars! But don't speak
so loud. It's supposed to be kept a great secret. I really oughtn't
to tell you at all!'

'But what is there to tell?' I whispered with satisfactory
impatience.

'You promise not to speak of it?'

'Of course!'

'Well, then, there are burglars in the neighbourhood.'

'Have they committed any robberies?'

'Not yet.'

'Then how do you know?'

'They've been seen. In the district. Two well-known London
thieves!'

Two! I looked at Raffles. I had done so often during the
evening, envying him his high spirits, his iron nerve, his
buoyant wit, his perfect ease and self-possession. But now I
pitied him; through all my own terror and consternation, I
pitied him as he sat eating and drinking, and laughing, and

talking, without a cloud of fear or of embarrassment on his handsome, taking, dare-devil face. I caught up my champagne and emptied the glass.

'Who has seen them?' I then asked calmly.

'A detective. They were traced down from town a few days ago. They are believed to have designs on the Abbey!'

'But why aren't they run in?'

'Exactly what I asked Papa on the way here this evening. He says there is no warrant out against the men at present, and all that can be done is to watch their movements.'

'Oh! so they are being watched?'

'Yes, by a detective who is down here on purpose. And I heard Lord Amersteth tell Papa that they had been seen this afternoon at Warbeck Junction.'

The very place where Raffles and I had been caught in the rain! Our stampede from the inn was now explained; on the other hand, I was no longer to be taken by surprise by anything that my companion might have to tell me; and I succeeded in looking her in the face with a smile.

'This is really quite exciting, Miss Melhuish,' said I. 'May I ask how you come to know so much about it?'

'It's Papa,' was the confidential reply. 'Lord Amersteth consulted him, and he consulted me. But for goodness' sake don't let it get about! I can't think what tempted me to tell you!'

'You may trust me, Miss Melhuish. But—aren't you frightened?' Miss Melhuish giggled.

'Not a bit! They won't come to the rectory. There's nothing for them there. But look round the table: look at the diamonds: look at old Lady Melrose's necklace alone!'

The Dowager-Marchioness of Melrose was one of the few persons whom it had been unnecessary to point out to me. She sat on Lord Amersteth's right, flourishing her ear-trumpet, and drinking champagne with her usual notorious freedom, as dissipated and kindly a dame as the world has ever seen. It was a necklace of diamonds and sapphires that rose and fell about her ample neck.

'They say it's worth five thousand pounds at least,' continued my companion. 'Lady Margaret told me so this morning (that's Lady Margaret next your Mr Raffles, you know); and the old dear will wear them every night. Think what a haul they would be! No; we don't feel in danger at the rectory.'

When the ladies rose, Miss Melhuish bound me to fresh vows of secrecy; and left me, I should think, with some remorse for her indiscretion, but more satisfaction at the importance which it had undoubtedly given her in my eyes. The opinion may smack of vanity, though, in reality, the very springs of conversation reside in that same human, universal itch to thrill the auditor. The peculiarity of Miss Melhuish was that she must be thrilling at all costs. And thrilling she had surely been.

I spare you my feelings of the next two hours. I tried hard to get a word with Raffles, but again and again I failed. In the dining-room he and Crowley lit their cigarettes with the same match, and had their heads together all the time. In the drawing-room I had the mortification of hearing him talk interminable nonsense into the trumpet-ear of Lady Melrose, whom he knew in town. Lastly, in the billiard-room, they had a great and lengthy pool, while I sat aloof and chafed more than ever in the company of a very serious Scotchman, who had arrived since dinner, and who would talk of nothing but the recent improvements in instantaneous photography. He had not come to play in the matches (he told me), but to obtain for Lord Amersteth such a series of cricket photographs as had never been taken before; whether as an amateur or a professional photographer I was unable to determine. I remember, however, seeking distraction in little bursts of resolute attention to the conversation of this bore. And so at last the long ordeal ended; glasses were emptied, men said good-night, and I followed Raffles to his room.

'It's all up!' I gasped, as he turned up the gas and I shut the door. 'We're being watched. We've been followed down from town. There's a detective here on the spot!'

'How do you know?' asked Raffles, turning upon me quite sharply, but without the least dismay. And I told him how I knew.

'Of course,' I added, 'it was the fellow we saw in the inn this afternoon.'

'The detective?' said Raffles. 'Do you mean to say you don't know a detective when you see one, Bunny?'

'If that wasn't the fellow, which is?'

Raffles shook his head.

'To think that you've been talking to him for the last hour in the billiard-room, and couldn't spot what he was!'

'The Scotch photographer—'

I paused aghast.

'Scotch he is,' said Raffles, 'and photographer he may be. He is also Inspector Mackenzie of Scotland Yard—the very man I sent the message to that night last April. And you couldn't spot who he was in a whole hour! Oh, Bunny, Bunny, you were never built for crime!'

'But,' said I, 'if that was Mackenzie, who was the fellow you bolted from at Warbeck?'

'The man he's watching.'

'But he's watching us!'

Raffles looked at me with a pitying eye, and shook his head again before handing me his open cigarette-case.

'I don't know whether smoking's forbidden in one's bed-room, but you'd better take one of these and stand tight, Bunny, because I'm going to say something offensive.'

I helped myself with a laugh.

'Say what you like, my dear fellow, if it really isn't you and I that Mackenzie's after.'

'Well, then, it isn't and it couldn't be, and nobody but a born Bunny would suppose for a moment that it was! Do you seriously think he would sit there and knowingly watch his man playing pool under his nose? Well, he might; he's a cool hand, Mackenzie; but I'm not cool enough to win a pool under such conditions. At least, I don't think I am; it would be interesting to see. The situation wasn't free from strain as it was, though I knew he wasn't thinking of us. Crowley told me all about it after dinner, you see, and then I'd seen one of the men for myself this afternoon. You thought it was a detective who made me turn tail at that inn. I really don't know why I didn't tell you at the time, but it was just the opposite. That loud, red-faced brute is one of the cleverest thieves in London, and I once had a drink with him and our mutual fence. I was an East-ender from tongue to toe at the moment, but you will understand that I don't run unnecessary risks of recognition by a brute like that.'

'He's not alone, I hear.'

'By no means; there's at least one other man with him; and it's suggested that there may be an accomplice here in the house.'

'Did Lord Crowley tell you so?'

'Crowley and the champagne between them. In confidence, of course, just as your girl told you; but even in confidence he never let on about Mackenzie. He told me there was a detective in the background, but that was all. Putting him up as a guest is evidently their big secret, to be kept from the other guests because it might offend them, but more particularly from the servants whom he's here to watch. That's my reading of the situation, Bunny, and you will agree with me that it's infinitely more interesting than we could have imagined it would prove.'

'But infinitely more difficult for us,' said I, with a sigh of pusillanimous relief. 'Our hands are tied for this week, at all events.'

'Not necessarily, my dear Bunny, though I admit that the chances are against us. Yet I'm not so sure of that either. There are all sorts of possibilities in these three-cornered combinations. Set A to watch B, and he won't have an eye left for C. That's the obvious theory, but then Mackenzie's a very big A. I should be sorry to have any boodle about me with that man in the house. Yet it would be great to nip in between A and B and score off them both at once! It would be worth a risk, Bunny, to do that; it would be worth risking something merely to take on old hands like B and his men at their own old game! Eh, Bunny? That would be something like a match. Gentlemen and Players at single wicket, by Jove!'

His eyes were brighter than I had known them for many a day. They shone with the perverted enthusiasm which was roused in him only by the contemplation of some new audacity. He kicked off his shoes and began pacing his room with noiseless rapidity; not since the night of the Old Bohemian dinner to Reuben Rosenthall had Raffles exhibited such excitement in my presence; and I was not sorry at the moment to be reminded of the fiasco to which that banquet had been the prelude.

'My dear A. J.,' said I in his very own tone, 'you're far too fond of the uphill game; you will eventually fall a victim to the sporting spirit and nothing else. Take a lesson from our last escape, and fly lower as you value our skins. Study the house as much as you like, but do—not—go and shove your head into Mackenzie's mouth!'

My wealth of metaphor brought him to a standstill, with his cigarette between his fingers and a grin beneath his shining eyes.

'You're quite right, Bunny. I won't. I really won't. Yet— you saw old Lady Melrose's necklace? I've been wanting it for years! But I'm not going to play the fool, honour bright, I'm not; yet—by Jove!—to get to windward of the professors and Mackenzie too! It would be a great game, Bunny, it would be a great game!'

'Well, you mustn't play it this week.'

'No, no, I won't. But I wonder how the professors think of going to work? That's what one wants to know. I wonder if they've really got an accomplice in the house? How I wish I knew their game! But it's all right, Bunny; don't you be jealous; it shall be as you wish.'

And with that assurance I went off to my own room and so to bed with an incredibly light heart. I had still enough of the honest man in me to welcome the postponement of our actual felonies, to dread their performance, to deplore their necessity: which is merely another way of stating the too patent fact that I was an incomparably weaker man than Raffles, while every whit as wicked. I had, however, one rather strong point. I possessed the gift of dismissing unpleasant considerations, not intimately connected with the passing moment, entirely from my mind. Through the exercise of this faculty I had lately been living my frivolous life in town with as much ignoble enjoyment as I had derived from it the year before; and similarly, here at Milchester, in the long-dreaded cricket week, I had after all a quite excellent time.

It is true that there were other factors in this pleasing disappointment. In the first place, *mirabile dictu*, there were one or two even greater duffers than I on the Abbey cricket field. Indeed, quite early in the week, when it was of most value to me, I gained considerable kudos for a lucky catch; a ball, of which I had merely heard the hum, stuck fast in my hand, which Lord Amersteth himself grasped in public congratulation. This happy accident was not to be undone even by me, and, as nothing succeeds like success, and the constant encouragement of the one great cricketer on the field was in itself an immense stimulus, I actually made a run or two in my very next innings. Miss Melhuish said pretty things to me that night at the great ball in honour of Viscount Crowley's majority; she also told me that was the night on which the robbers would assuredly make their raid, and was full of arch tremors when we sat out in the garden, though the entire premises were illuminated all night long. Meanwhile the quiet Scotchman took countless photographs by day, which he developed by night in a darkroom admirably situated in the servants' part of the house; and it is my firm belief that only two of his fellow guests knew Mr Clephane of Dundee for Inspector Mackenzie of Scotland Yard.

The week was to end with a trumpery match on the Saturday, which two or three of us intended abandoning early in order to return to town that night. The match, however, was never played. In the small hours of the Saturday morning a tragedy took place at Milchester Abbey.

Let me tell of the thing as I saw and heard it. My room opened upon the central gallery, and was not even on the same floor as that on which Raffles—and I think all the other men— were quartered. I had been put, in fact, into the dressing-room of one of the grand suites, and my two near neighbours were old Lady Melrose and my host and hostess. Now, by the Friday evening the actual festivities were at an end, and, for the first time that week, I must have been sound asleep since midnight, when all at once I found myself sitting up breathless. A heavy thud had come against my door, and now I heard hard breathing and the dull stamp of muffled feet.

'I've got ye,' muttered a voice. 'It's no use struggling.'

It was the Scotch detective, and a new fear turned me cold. There was no reply, but the hard breathing grew harder still, and the muffled feet beat the floor to a quicker measure. In sudden panic I sprang out of bed and flung open my door. A light burnt low on the landing, and by it I could see Mackenzie swaying and staggering in a silent tussle with some powerful adversary.

'Hold this man!' he cried, as I appeared. 'Hold the rascal!'

But I stood like a fool until the pair of them backed into me, when, with a deep breath, I flung myself on the fellow, whose face I had seen at last. He was one of the footmen who waited at table; and no sooner had I pinned him than the detective loosed his hold.

'Hang on to him,' he cried. 'There's more of 'em below.'

And he went leaping down the stairs, as other doors opened and Lord Amersteth and his son appeared simultaneously in their pyjamas. At that my man ceased struggling; but I was still holding him when Crowley turned up the gas.

'What the devil's all this?' asked Lord Amersteth, blinking. 'Who was that ran downstairs?'

'Mac—Clephane!' said I hastily.

'Aha!' said he, turning to the footman. 'So you're the scoundrel, are you?—Well done! Well done! Where was he caught?'

I had no idea.

'Here's Lady Melrose's door open,' said Crowley.—'Lady Melrose! Lady Melrose!'

'You forget she's deaf,' said Lord Amersteth. 'Ah! that'll be her maid.'

An inner door had opened; next instant there was a little shriek, and a white figure gesticulated on the threshold.

'*Où donc est l'écrin de Madame la Marquise? La fenêtre est ouverte. Il a disparu!*'

'Window open and jewel-case gone, by Jove!' exclaimed Lord Amersteth. '*Mais comment est Madame la Marquise? Est-elle bien?*'

'*Oui, milor. Elle dort.*'

'Sleeps through it all,' said my lord. 'She's the only one, then!'

'What made Mackenzie—Clephane—bolt?' young Crowley asked me.

'Said there were more of them below.'

'Why the devil couldn't you tell us so before?' he cried, and went leaping downstairs in his turn.

He was followed by nearly all the cricketers, who now burst upon the scene in a body, only to desert it for the chase. Raffles was one of them, and I would gladly have been another, had not the footman chosen this moment to hurl me from him, and to make a dash in the direction from which they had come. Lord Amersteth had him in an instant; but the fellow fought desperately, and it took the two of us to drag him downstairs, amid a terrified chorus from half-open doors. Eventually we handed him over to two other footmen who appeared with their night-shirts tucked into their trousers, and my host was good enough to compliment me as he led the way outside.

'I though I heard a shot,' he added. 'Didn't you?'

'I thought I heard three.'

And out we dashed into the darkness.

I remember how the gravel pricked my feet, how the wet grass numbed them as we made for the sound of voices on an outlying lawn. So dark was the night that we were in the cricketers' midst before we saw the shimmer of their pyjamas, and then Lord Amersteth almost trod on Mackenzie as he lay prostrate in the dew.

'Who's this?' he cried. 'What on earth's happened?'

'It's Clephane,' said a man who knelt over him. 'He's got a bullet in him somewhere.'

'Is he alive?'

'Barely.'

'Good God! Where's Crowley?'

'Here I am,' called a breathless voice. 'It's no good, you fellows. There's nothing to show which way they've gone. Here's Raffles; he's chucked it, too.' And they ran up panting.

'Well, we've got one of them, at all events,' muttered Lord Amersteth. 'The next thing is to get this poor fellow indoors. Take his shoulders, somebody. Now his middle. Join hands under him. All together now; that's the way. Poor fellow! Poor fellow! His name isn't Clephane at all. He's a Scotland Yard detective, down here for these very villains!'

Raffles was the first to express surprise; but he had also been the first to raise the wounded man. Nor had any of them a stronger or more tender hand in the slow procession to the house. In a little we had the senseless man stretched on a sofa in the library. And there, with ice on his wound and brandy in his throat, his eyes opened and his lips moved.

Lord Amersteth bent down to catch the words.

'Yes, yes,' said he; 'we've got one of them safe and sound. The brute you collared upstairs.' Lord Amersteth bent lower. 'By Jove! Lowered the jewel-case out of the window, did he? And they've got clean away with it. Well, well! I only hope we'll be able to pull this good fellow through. He's off again.'

An hour passed: the sun was rising.

It found a dozen young fellows on the settees in the billiard-room, drinking whisky and soda-water in their overcoats and pyjamas, and still talking excitedly in one breath. A time-table was being passed from hand to hand: the doctor was still in the library. At last the door opened, and Lord Amersteth put in his head.

'It isn't hopeless,' said he, 'but it's bad enough. There'll be no cricket today.'

Another hour, and most of us were on our way to catch the early train; between us we filled a compartment almost to suffocation. And still we talked all together of the night's event; and still I was a little hero in my way, for having kept my hold of the one ruffian who had been taken; and my gratification was subtle and intense. Raffles watched me under lowered lids. Not a word had we had together; not a word did we have until we had left the others at Paddington, and were skimming through the streets in a hansom with noiseless tyres and a tinkling bell.

'Well, Bunny,' said Raffles, 'so the professors have it, eh?'

'Yes,' said I. 'And I'm jolly glad!'

'That poor Mackenzie has a ball in his chest?'

'That you and I have been on the decent side for once.'

He shrugged his shoulders.

'You're hopeless, Bunny, quite hopeless! I take it you wouldn't have refused your share if the boodle had fallen to us? Yet you positively enjoy coming off second best—for the second time running! I confess, however, that the professors' methods were full of interest to me. I, for one, have probably gained as much in experience as I have lost in other things. That lowering the jewelcase out of the window was a very simple and effective expedient; two of them had been waiting below for it for hours.'

'How do you know?' I asked.

'I saw them from my own window, which was just above the dear old lady's. I was fretting for that necklace in particular, when I went up to turn in for our last night—and I happened to look out of the window. In point of fact, I wanted to see whether the one below was open, and whether there was the slightest chance of working the oracle with my sheet for a rope. Of course I took the precaution of turning my light off first, and it was a lucky thing I did. I saw the pros. right down below, and they never saw me. I saw a little tiny luminous disc just for an instant, and then again for an instant a few minutes later. Of course I knew what it was, for I have my own watch-dial daubed with luminous paint; it makes a lantern of sorts when you can get no better. But these fellows were not using theirs as a lantern. They were under the old lady's window. They were watching the time. The whole thing was arranged with their accomplice inside. Set a thief to catch a thief: in a minute I had guessed what the whole thing proved to be.'

'And you did nothing!' I exclaimed.

'On the contrary, I went downstairs and straight into Lady Melrose's room——'

'You did?'

'Without a moment's hesitation. To save her jewels. And I was prepared to yell as much into her ear-trumpet for all the house to hear. But the dear lady is too deaf and too fond of her dinner to wake easily.'

'Well?'

'She didn't stir.'

'And yet you allowed the professors, as you call them, to take her jewels, case and all!'

'All but this,' said Raffles, thrusting his fist into my lap. 'I would have shown it you before, but really, old fellow, your face all day has been worth a fortune to the firm!'

And he opened his fist, to shut it next instant on the bunch of diamonds and of sapphires that I had last seen encircling the neck of Lady Melrose.

8 *Some Memories of the Nineteen-twenties*

R. C. ROBERTSON-GLASGOW

I PLAYED a walking-on part in my first match for Somerset, against Hampshire at Taunton, bowling third change with a mottled ball against that monumental left-hander, Philip Mead. In the second innings he made 176 not out. The Hampshire captain, L. H. (now Lord) Tennyson, and his valet-wicket-keeper, Walter Livesey, had three O's between them in four innings, the proportion being two to the master and one to the man. Tennyson was caught off Jack White each time. Each year he swore that he would hit Jack for six at Taunton, but the ground is just that little bigger than it looks, and down she used to come into the deep-fielder's hands.

Tennyson missed the poetry of his Laureate grandfather but inherited the constitution and the plain private speech. No stronger or bolder player of the forward stroke was seen in his day. He received the fast bowlers as the oak receives the storm; and, when he fell to them, he went down with no grace or compliancy, but with a sounding, defiant crash. In the next summer, 1921, he fixed his name for ever among storied cricketers, showing his fading companions how to face Gregory and McDonald and, one-handed, smacking them for 63 and 35 in the third Test at Leeds. In all ways of cricket and the world he was and is the perfect English Gascon, a gourmet of the whole feast of life which, for him, has been post-dated by a century and a half. He was cut out for the Regency. Lionel should have been the ancestor; Alfred the descendant.

And so to the return match with Hampshire, at Bournemouth, which was under the dyarchy of bath-chairs and Dan Godfrey. I spent the evening before it exploring with Jack MacBryan. I wonder how many of those who chance to see his name in cricket scores remember what a great player Jack

93

MacB. was? In 1920, he struggled to a Blue at Cambridge. Four years later, he played as opening batsman for England against South Africa, being chosen from a field of openers that included Jack Hobbs, Herbert Sutcliffe, George Gunn, Jack (A. C.) Russell, Andrew Sandham, and Charles Hallows, all of them rightaway professional topsawyers. MacBryan had been a Prisoner of War with the Germans during much of the Kaiser's war, and had been awarded a spell of solitary confinement for using a *soi-disant* pudding as a Rugger ball.

That evening, Jack was in one of those moods of *en-tout-cas* preparedness in which a man tends to laugh at the morrow and criticize other people's hats. Soon after leaving the hotel, we were nearly run over by a car which, Jack remarked, was probably in the pay of the Hampshire Committee. At the next corner, the same thing happened. Jack MacB. shouted one of those terms calculated to cause all but the more experienced London taxi-drivers to draw up within a few lengths. There followed an altercation with the charioteer, whose fondness for alcohol was now manifest. Jack drew off his coat, but there the matter rested. As the driver receded, taking what revenge he could out of the gears, Jack turned to me and said: 'Good. Now I'll make a hundred.' And he did.

So did John Daniell; a solid, wearing-down innings, at which he excelled. Sometimes he had fits of thinking he was Jessop, and would be comfortably caught at long-leg. And when he holed out, he was apt to ask why 'that ruddy captain can't keep his fielders where he put 'em'.

We won that match; and I took five Hampshire wickets in their first innings, using the inswerve; and John Daniell told me that no batsman worth a sausage ever got out to inswervers, overlooking, in his disciplinary zeal, his own fate at Oxford two months earlier. Young bowler, don't be put off by the wisdom of the elders! Whichever way you bowl, they'll tell you of a better way. You and you alone will know whether you've bowled like a king or a cow. And, in cricket, the bowlers are the Lords and the batsmen are the Commoners;

and you'll find that, as in politics, it's not the Lords who get the Press.

The great Len Braund was then in his last season but one for Somerset. It was twenty years since he had been the greatest all-round cricketer in the world, classic batsman, a destroyer with his leg-breaks, and a slip-fielder who could pick 'em off his toes while discussing the Derby with the wicket-keeper. He was, and is, the wisest judge of cricket I know. He could tell you, as no other, just what to try, against whom, and when. By 1920 he had stopped bowling, except a casual spinner between the fall of wickets, and, for batting, he preferred high noon to the shades of evening. At slip, he was catching the snorters. The easy ones he was apt to leave for the grass.

Now he has passed the three-score-and-ten, but his heart is still seventeen; and he treats his artificial legs as interesting interlopers. He told me how, as he lay in hospital soon after an amputation, he had what he referred to as a natural call, but found the ward temporarily nurse-less. 'So,' he said, 'I got up, got there, and got back. But, as I was doing the last hop or so, the nurse came in, and said: "Mr Braund, what on earth do you think you're trying to do?" And I couldn't help thinking of the time Mr Daniell said the same thing to me when I floored one in the slips. Only he didn't say "on earth".'

H. C. McDonell, who bowled slowish tempters, was in that Hampshire side. He fielded to his own bowling like a red-hot jack-in-the-box, in the attitude of a man trying to catch butterflies in both hands at once. He broke his finger catching-and-bowling Frank Woolley in the first county match I ever saw, at Canterbury, when C. B. Fry made a hundred in each innings and wore a huge white sun-hat. How easy it is to play the House-that-Jack-Built with the cricket generations. It was Fry's vote, though he did not know it or so intend it, which removed W. G. Grace from the England captaincy and team in 1899. And W. G. Grace was being shown a cricket bat by his mother at Thornbury while the Duke of Wellington was still alive; though what the Duke has to do with cricket I'm bothered if I know.

So, the match was over and we'd won. And our stock bowler, Ernest Robson, drank a pint of beer, curled his moustache, lit his pipe, and made as if to offer me a remark; but as usual found himself unequal to it, and walked thoughtfully from the ground.

And, I being nineteen, rushed away for an evening paper to see what they said about my bowling. They said that the Hampshire batsmen had failed unaccountably against an attack that presented no obvious difficulty.

Unaccountably? No obvious difficulty? Nuts.

There followed a defeat at Lord's by Middlesex, who were on that great spurt to the Championship under 'Plum' Warner. And so to the Weston-super-Mare Festival. Of all county grounds, Clarence Park, Weston-super-Mare, is about the smallest and the most intimate. It was the home pitch of Jim Bridges, Somerset bowler, and there in club matches, he liked to come out strong as a batsman. 'If only they *knew*,' he used to tell me, 'that you and I, Glasgie, are as good batsmen as any in the Somerset side . . . except, possibly, Dah Lyon and Jack MacBryan.' But this knowledge was somehow kept from our captain, who used to say: 'Well, you two clowns can toss for who goes in ten or eleven.' Jim never would toss, but took number ten with an air of injury and neglect. After all, the year before, he'd made 99 not out against Essex on his native sward; mostly by huge high balloons.

The Weston ground in August was a thing of marquees where the right stuff could be found, and deck chairs and wooden chairs under which the spade and bucket could be parked for an hour or two. In those days the pitch was sportive, having sea sand close under the grass, and in the three matches of 1920 only once was a total of 200 reached in 11 completed innings. A short walk away from the ground were the golf-links, where Secretary Bob Riddell held sway. Bob was a left-hand golfer of much skill, and as a host he had no equal. He could produce you golf shoes from nowhere, and a complete change of clothing in rain-storms. There, peace was to be found in the evening, balm for any failure on the cricket field; and in the lounge, Doctor MacBryan, Jack's father, would be sitting, benevolent and conversational, in a drain-pipe collar that kept stiff up to his ears. Something odd always happened at Weston-super-Mare. It was there, in a hotel, that P. G. H. Fender, the Surrey captain, complained to the manager that there wasn't enough room in the bedrooms to swing a cat, and the manager told Percy Fender that he didn't know they'd come down to Weston merely for the cat-swinging.

We lost to Leicestershire in the first match of the Festival. It was a bad batting match, especially for the older gentlemen, our Ernest Robson and their J. H. King, ninety-five years between them, making only 1 run in their 4 innings. King made up for it by doing the hat-trick in our second innings. The third wicket of the feat being also his hundredth of the season. He was surrounded by congratulations; and his face was illuminated by triumph, as I walked to the crease, a possible fourth in hand. But I corrected his exuberance by hitting my first ball out of the ground and over the pavilion at mid-wicket. I added one more, then was feebly caught and bowled by Ewart Astill. In the Leicestershire second innings I took 5 for 33, and caught G. B. F. Rudd, 71, in the deep field with a sound like a bag bursting.

John King, of Leicestershire, left-hand bat and bowler, went on playing for the county till he was fifty-four years old. In 1904, brought into the Players' side at Lord's as a substitute for J. T. Tyldesley, he scored a century in each innings. In his latter years he was a slowish mover between the wickets, and once, being run out at Leicester by many yards while facing the right way for the pavilion, he was told by umpire Reeves to 'keep on running, John, while your legs are loose'. John was very angry about this.

We lost the next match, against Essex, for whom there was playing an enormous man, P. Toone. He was a tremendous thrower, but wild, and once threw the ball from the deep field clean over the wicket-keeper's head against the far screen. He seemed well pleased with this feat. I made 15 not out, out of 99, and 22 out of 160. Hot going, I thought; and in the next match, against Derbyshire, I was promoted to number eight, much to the disgust of Jim Bridges. But as I scored 21, he couldn't say much. We beat Derbyshire by 10 wickets, Jack White, the greatest slow left-hand bowler Somerset ever had, taking 12 for 79. John Daniell scored 102 in the first innings, and was very severe on the off-spinner, Arthur Morton, sweeping him again and again to the leg boundary and reaching his 50 in less than half an hour.

Arthur Morton was a sturdy all-rounder, and later became a first-class umpire. When standing umpire some years after this, he called several no-balls against a certain West Indies fast bowler. The excitable victim, resenting these attentions, revenged himself by running towards the wicket, knocking Morton flat on his face, and shouting: 'Was THAT a no-ball, then?' Apologies were made; Morton straightened his teeth and scraped the grass from his eyebrows, and the game proceeded.

So ended the season 1920. I finished with 55 wickets at 20.90 each, and John Daniell asked me to play again next year, adding the request, 'and for heaven's sake, don't bring that bloody straw-hat'.

Almost nothing, except the sunshine, went right with Oxford cricket in 1921. Technically, this was hard to explain. Of the 1920 team, we had lost only three, F. W. Gilligan, F. A. Waldock, and C. H. L. Skeet. But neither Bettington nor Stevens bowled as skilfully as they had done the summer before, and, as to me, I took on a transitional shape in which I was increasing speed and casting away the habit of the inswing. Probably, I ought to have stayed in the nets and had it all out on my own. Our captain, V. R. Price, was an erratic, occasionally a brilliant, fast bowler, but, somehow, we were never a whole cricket side; just a collection of individuals playing cricket.

Against such a side as Cambridge in 1921, this was just asking for defeat. And we had it. They won by an innings and 24 runs.

That Cambridge team was just about the best University eleven that went to Lord's in my memory. They batted thus, in brackets being the runs scored in the only innings that they found necessary: J. L. Bryan (62), C. A. Fiddian-Green (17), G. Ashton (12), H. Ashton (118), A. P. F. Chapman (45), C. T. Ashton (48), M. D. Lyon (9), A. G. Doggart (45), C. H. Gibson (43 not out), R. G. Evans (0 not out), C. S. Marriott did not bat.

Gilbert Ashton was captain. Their opening bowlers were Clem Gibson, of England quality, and R. G. Evans, very accurate and capable of both swerves. To follow, they had 'Father' Marriott, one of the finest slow bowlers who ever played in the 'Varsity match, and Graham Doggart, a sturdy stock bowler who could nip them in awkwardly from the off.

In batting, they had that rare and enviable mixture of the sound and the brilliant. Jack Bryan was sound, and also left-handed. His partner, Charles Fiddian-Green, was the very mirror of orthodoxy, and, further, an all-round games-player of unusual ability, reaching the first-class at cricket, rugby, golf, and hockey. Sartorially, he was the Beau Brummell of the side. The three Ashtons between them provided all the known strokes of the right-hander. Percy Chapman, on his own, already approached Frank Woolley in all but sheer grace. M. D. Lyon, powerful and aggressive, was soon to become the stay of Somerset; and when these had made their runs, there was Doggart, who was good enough to bat at number three in most 'Varsity teams. To crown all, they won the toss.

In fielding, they were the one team in England that year who could compare with W. W. Armstrong's Australians. At shortleg, Hubert Ashton had no superior. At cover-point, there was Percy Chapman. Some years later, Chapman set a new standard in the gully; but that was when his legs were heavier

99

and his frame set. At cover, in lithe and pliable youth, he was a non-pareil. Nothing stoppable seemed to escape his huge hands and telescopic reach; being left-handed, he could pounce on those balls that swerve away from cover towards third-man, and, still stooping, he would flick them back over the bails.

As a batsman, Chapman was something different from the other very good ones who were—just very good. His great reach, keenness of eye, and exceptional strength of wrist and forearm made him a murderous opponent. In later years, even while he was still captain of England, he had curtailed his full swing of the bat. He learnt cunning and what to leave alone. But, in his Cambridge days he used no cunning, no more than Coeur de Lion would have used it when knocking off some Saracen's head, and he left nothing alone. It was plain, when you bowled to him, that he believed himself able to score off anything, felt himself to be master of the whole armoury of the bowler's attack. And, when you put one past him, he didn't retract from that view or attitude, but thought 'my mistake', not 'your good ball'. On and just outside the off stump he had those delayed strokes that defy description, half cut and half drive, and it didn't matter how good was the length of the ball. He never had the defence of Frank Woolley; very few have had that; but he was a stronger man, far, and you noticed it when fielding at cover-point. Chapman and records somehow don't pair together, but he is the only man who has brought off the 'treble' at Lord's, of a century in the University match, for Gentlemen v. Players, and for England v. Australia.

They dropped him from the England captaincy soon after that century against Australia; and the Australians could hardly be persuaded of their wonderful luck. As a captain, he was the best I have known. He had the flair. He could encourage by a gesture or a look, and he had the whole confidence of the whole side. The critics talk of Archie MacLaren, and Noble, and W. G. Grace as leaders. But results can talk as well; and Chapman captained England in six consecutive victories against Australia. And that's another record. But he had so much that defeats words and the pen; gaiety, freedom, hope, enjoyment. In him was gathered all that makes cricket worth playing.

In the 'Varsity match, Hubert Ashton batted beautifully for his 118, and Douglas Jardine, having Chapman caught and bowling Doggart, surprised both friend and foe. For Oxford, Ward and Hedges made some runs in each innings, Holdsworth some lovely strokes in the first. As in 1920. A. F. Bickmore batted with distinction, and it was sad that his 57 should have been ended by a long-hop. I thought I bowled well, and had Chapman missed at wicket before he had scored, but the wickets wouldn't fall, and Geoffrey Lowndes rebuked me for gesticulating when they nearly did.

Meanwhile, the Australians, with J. M. Gregory and E. A. McDonald as their spearhead of attack, were knocking the dust out of English cricket. Their captain, Warwick W. Armstrong, was now in his forty-third year and weighed at least seventeen stone. He was the nearest thing to W. G. Grace that Australia had produced, both in bulk and ability. He somewhat resembled the Old Man in his method of bowling, rolling the ball from leg for as long as you pleased, with a sort of comfortable assiduity and strainless guile. As a batsman, he had become rather slow of foot, but he still drove with great power, and could stick at need.

As a captain, Armstrong was reckoned among the astutest of tacticians; but it must be admitted that, in 1921, he was not called upon to exercise any exceptional ingenuity, for what Gregory and McDonald left, Arthur Mailey mopped up. Armstrong was not a man of many words, but the few that he uttered were apt to be noticed. He crossed ideas with the MCC at the very start of the tour, demanding a change in the programme to allow the Australians a day's rest before each Test match. This reasonable request caused an uneasy stir in the sanctuary.

The truth was, English cricket was in sore and crusty mood, like an old gentleman who has received a caning. There was another disagreement, humorous enough, if humour were

101

appreciated in the high places of cricket. Armstrong asked that drinks should be served in the dressing-room at Lord's. F. E. (later Sir Francis) Lacey, the Secretary of MCC, said that the bar downstairs was the only and proper place for liquid re-freshment. But Armstrong carried his point. These pin-pricks made sore relations, and, when Gregory and McDonald began to make free with the rather timorous remains of England batting, there were not wanting those who said there was some-thing unfair in the bowling. They objected to their old men being knocked about. In result, Armstrong passed as something of an ogre in cricket that summer, and the climax was reached in the Fifth Test, at the Oval, when Armstrong, fielding in front of the pavilion, trapped a wind-swept newspaper under his large boot, and read it. He said that the racing news was more interesting than the cricket provided.

9 *A Country Cricket-match*

MARY RUSSELL MITFORD

I DOUBT if there be any scene in the world more animating or delightful than a cricket-match—I do not mean a set match at Lord's Ground, for money, hard money, between a certain number of gentlemen and players, as they are called—people who make a trade of that noble sport, and degrade it into an affair of bettings, and hedgings and cheatings, it may be, like boxing or horse-racing; nor do I mean a pretty fête in a gentleman's park, where one club of cricketing dandies encounter another such club, and where they show off in graceful costume to a gay marquee of admiring belles, who condescend so to purchase admiration, and while away a long summer morning in partaking cold collations, conversing occasionally, and seeming to understand the game—the whole being conducted according to ball-room etiquette, so as to be exceedingly elegant and exceedingly dull. No! the cricket that I mean is a real solid old-fashioned match between neighbouring parishes, where each attacks the other for honour and a supper, glory and half-a-crown a man. If there be any gentlemen amongst them, it is well—if not, it is so much the better. Your gentleman cricketer is in general rather an anomalous character. Elderly gentlemen are obviously good for nothing; and your beaux are, for the most part, hampered and trammelled by dress and habit; the stiff cravat, the pinched-in-waist, the dandy-walk—oh, they will never do for cricket! Now, our country lads, accustomed to the flail or the hammer (your blacksmiths are capital hitters) have the free use of their arms; they know how to move their shoulders; and they can move their feet too—they can run; then they are so much better made, so much more athletic, and yet so much lissimer—to use a Hampshire phrase, which deserves at least to be good English.

Here and there, indeed, one meets with an old Etonian, who retains his boyish love for that game which formed so considerable a branch of his education; some even preserve their boyish proficiency, but in general it wears away like the Greek, quite as certainly, and almost as fast; a few years of Oxford, or Cambridge, or the Continent, are sufficient to annihilate both the power and the inclination. No! a village match is the thing —where our highest officer—our conductor (to borrow a musical term) is but a little farmer's second son; where a day-labourer is our bowler, and a blacksmith our long-stop; where the spectators consist of the retired cricketers, the veterans of the green, the careful mothers, the girls, and all the boys of two parishes, together with a few amateurs, little above them in rank, and not at all in pretension; where laughing and shouting, and the very ecstasy of merriment and good-humour prevail: such a match, in short, as I attended yesterday, at the expense of getting twice wet through, and as I would attend tomorrow, at the certainty of having that ducking doubled.

For the last three weeks our village has been in a state of great excitement, occasioned by a challenge from our north-western neighbours, the men of B., to contend with us at cricket. Now, we have not been much in the habit of playing matches. Three or four years ago, indeed, we encountered the men of S., our neighbours south-by-east, with a sort of doubtful success, beating them on our own ground, whilst they in the second match returned the compliment on theirs. This discouraged us. Then an unnatural coalition between a high-church curate and an evangelical gentleman-farmer drove our lads from the Sunday-even practice, which, as it did not begin before both services were concluded, and as it tended to keep the young men from the ale-house, our magistrates had winked at if not encouraged. The sport, therefore, had languished until the present season, when under another change of circumstances the spirit began to revive. Half-a-dozen fine active lads, of influence amongst their comrades, grew into men and yearned for cricket; an enterprising publican gave a set of ribands: his rival, mine host of the Rose, and out-doer by profession, gave two; and the clergyman and his lay ally, both well-disposed and good-natured men, gratified by the sub-mission to their authority, and finding, perhaps, that no great good resulted from the substitution of public houses for out-of-doors diversions, relaxed. In short, the practice re-com-menced, and the hill was again alive with men and boys, and innocent merriment; but farther than the riband matches amongst ourselves nobody dreamed of going, till this challenge —we were modest, and doubted our own strength. The B. people, on the other hand, must have been braggers born, a whole parish of gasconaders. Never was such boasting! such crowing! such ostentatious display of practice! such mutual compliments from man to man—bowler to batter, batter to bowler! It was a wonder they did not challenge all England. It must be confessed that we were a little astounded; yet we firmly resolved not to decline the combat; and one of the most spirited of the new growth, William Grey by name, took up the glove in a style of manly courtesy, that would have done honour to a knight in the days of chivalry—'We were not pro-fessed players,' he said, 'being little better than school-boys, and scarcely older; but, since they have done us the honour to challenge us, we would try our strength. It would be no dis-credit to be beaten by such a field.'

Having accepted the wager of battle, our champion began forthwith to collect his forces. William Grey is himself one of the finest youths that one shall see—tall, active, slender and yet strong, with a piercing eye full of sagacity, and a smile full of good honour—a farmer's son by station, and used to hard work as farmers' sons are now, liked by everybody, and admitted to be an excellent cricketer. He immediately set forth to muster his men, remembering with great complacency that Samuel Long, a bowler *comme il y en a peu*, the very man who had knocked down nine wickets, had beaten us, bowled us out at the fatal return match some years ago at S., had luckily, in a remove of a quarter of a mile last Ladyday, crossed the boundaries of his old parish, and actually belonged to us. Here was a stroke of good fortune! Our captain applied to him instantly; and he agreed at a word. Indeed, Samuel Long is a very civilized person. He is a middle-aged man, who looks rather old amongst our young lads, and whose thickness and breadth gave no token of remarkable activity; but he is very active, and so steady a player! so safe! We had half gained the match when we had secured him. He is a man of substance, too, in every way; owns one cow, two donkeys, six pigs, and geese and ducks beyond count—dresses like a farmer, and owes no man a shilling—and all this from pure industry, sheer day-labour. Note that your good cricketer is commonly the most industrious man in the parish; the habits that make him such are precisely those which make a good workman—steadiness, sobriety, and activity—Samuel Long might pass for the beau ideal of the two characters. Happy were we to possess him! Then we had another piece of good luck. James Brown, a journeyman blacksmith and a native, who, being of a rambling disposition, had roamed from place to place for half-a-dozen years, had just returned to settle with his brother at another corner of our village, bringing with him a prodigious reputation in cricket and in gallantry—the gay Lothario of the neighbourhood. He is said to have made more conquests in love and in cricket than any blacksmith in the county. To him also went the indefatigable William Grey, and he also consented to play. No end to our good fortune! Another celebrated batter, called Joseph Hearne, had likewise recently married into the parish. He worked, it is true at the A. mills, but slept at the house of his wife's father in our territories. He also was sought and found by our leader. But he was grand and shy; made an immense favour of the thing; courted courting and then hung back—'Did not know that he could be spared; had partly resolved not to play again—at least not this season; thought it rash to accept the challenge; thought they might do without

106

him—' 'Truly I think so too,' said our spirited champion; 'we will not trouble you, Mr Hearne.'

Having thus secured two powerful auxiliaries and rejected a third, we began to reckon and select the regular native forces. Thus ran our list: William Grey, 1—Samuel Long, 2—James Brown, 3—George and John Simmons, one capital the other so-so—an uncertain hitter, but a good fieldsman, 5—Joel Brent, excellent, 6—Ben Appleton—here was a little pause—Ben's abilities at cricket was not completely ascertained; but then he was so good a fellow, so full of fun and waggery! no doing without Ben. So he figured in the list, 7—George Harris—a short halt there too! Slowish—slow but sure. I think the proverb brought him in, 8—Tom Coper—Oh, beyond the world, Tom Coper! the red-headed gardening lad, whose left-handed strokes send *her* (a cricket-ball, like that other moving thing, a ship, is always of the feminine gender), send her spinning a mile, 9—Harry Willis, another blacksmith, 10.

We had now ten of our eleven, but the choice of the last occasioned some demur. Three young Martins, rich farmers of the neighbourhood, successively presented themselves, and were all rejected by our independent and impartial general for want of merit—cricketal merit. 'Not good enough,' was his pithy answer. Then our worthy neighbour, the half-pay lieutenant, offered his services—he, too, though with some hesitation and modesty, was refused—'Not quite young enough' was his sentence. John Strong, the exceeding long son of our dwarfish mason, was the next candidate—a nice youth—everybody likes John Strong—and a willing, but so tall and so limp, bent in the middle—a threadpaper, six feet high! We were all afraid that, in spite of his name, his strength would never hold out. 'Wait till next year, John,' quoth William Grey, with all the dignified seniority of twenty speaking to eighteen. 'Coper's a year younger,' said John. 'Coper's a foot shorter,' replied William: so John retired: and the eleventh man remained unchosen, almost to the eleventh hour. The eve of the match arrived, and the post was still vacant, when a little boy of fifteen, David Willis, brother to Harry, admitted by accident to the last practice, saw eight of them out, and was voted in by acclamation.

That Sunday evening's practice (for Monday was the important day) was a period of great anxiety, and, to say the truth, of great pleasure. There is something strangely delightful in the innocent spirit of party. To be one of a numerous body, to be authorized to say *we*, to have a rightful interest in triumph or

defeat, is gratifying at once to social feeling and to personal pride. There was not a ten-year-old urchin, or a septuagenary woman in the parish who did not feel an additional importance, a reflected consequence, in speaking of 'our side'. An election interests in the same way; but that feeling is less pure. Money is there, and hatred, and politics, and lies. Oh, to be a voter, or a voter's wife, comes nothing near the genuine and hearty sympathy of belonging to a parish, breathing the same air, looking on the same trees, listening to the same nightingales! Talk of a patriotic elector! Give me a parochial patriot, a man who loves his parish. Even we, the female partisans, may partake the common ardour. I am sure I did. I never, though tolerably eager and enthusiastic at all times, remember being in a more delicious state of excitement than on the eve of that battle. Our hopes waxed stronger and stronger. Those of our players who were present were excellent. William Grey got forty notches off his own bat, and that brilliant hitter, Tom Coper, gained eight from two successive balls. As the evening

advanced, too, we had encouragement of another sort. A spy, who had been despatched to reconnoitre the enemy's quarters, returned from their practising ground with a most consolatory report. 'Really,' said Charles Grover, our intelligence—a fine old steady judge, one who had played well in his day—'they are no better than so many old women. Any five of ours would beat their eleven.' This sent us to bed in high spirits.

Morning dawned less favourably. The sky promised a series of deluging showers, and kept its word as English skies are wont to do on such occasions; and a lamentable message arrived at the head-quarters from our trusty comrade Joel Brent. His master, a great farmer, had begun the hay-harvest that very morning, and Joel, being as eminent in one field as in another, could not be spared. Imagine Joel's plight! the most ardent of all our eleven! a knight held back from the tourney! a soldier from the battle! The poor swain was inconsolable. At last, one who is always ready to do a good-natured action, great or little, set forth to back his petition; and, by dint of appealing to the public spirit of our worthy neighbour and the state of the barometer, talking alternately of the parish honour and thunder showers, of last matches and sopped hay, he carried his point, and returned triumphantly with the delighted Joel.

In the meantime, we became sensible of another defalcation. On calling over our roll, Brown was missing; and the spy of the preceding night, Charles Grover—the universal scout and messenger of the village, a man who will run half-a-dozen miles for a pint of beer, who does errands for the very love of the trade, who, if he had been a lord, would have been an ambassador—was instantly despatched to summon the truant. His report spread general consternation. Brown had set off at four o'clock in the morning to play in a cricket-match at M., a little town twelve miles off, which had been his last residence. Here was desertion! Here was treachery! Here was treachery against that goodly state, our parish! To send James Brown to Coventry was the immediate resolution; but even that seemed too light a punishment for such delinquency! Then how we cried him down! At ten on Sunday night (for the rascal had actually practised with us, and never said a word of his intended disloyalty) he was our faithful mate, and the best player (take him all in all) of the eleven. At ten in the morning he had run away, and we were well rid of him; he was no batter compared with William Grey or Tom Coper; not fit to wipe the shoes of Samuel Long, as a bowler; nothing of a scout to John Simmons; the boy David Willis was worth fifty of him—

I trust we have within our realm
Five hundred good as he

was the universal sentiment. So we took tall John Strong, who, with an incurable hankering after the honour of being admitted, had kept constantly with the players, to take the chance of some such accident—we took John for our *pis aller*. I never saw anyone prouder than the good-humoured lad was of this not very flattering piece of preferment.

John Strong was elected, and Brown sent to Coventry; and when I first heard of his delinquency, I thought the punishment only too mild for the crime. But I have since learned the secret history of the offence (if we could know the secret histories of all offences, how much better the world would seem than it does now!) and really my wrath is much abated. It was a piece of gallantry, of devotion to the sex, or rather a chivalrous obedience to one chosen fair. I must tell my readers the story. Mary Allen, the prettiest girl of M., had, it seems, revenged upon our blacksmith the numberless inconsistencies of which he stood accused. He was in love over head and ears, but the nymph was cruel. She said no, and no, and no, and poor Brown, three times rejected, at last resolved to leave the place, partly in despair, and partly in the hope which often mingles strangely with a lover's despair, the hope that when he was gone he should be missed. He came home to his brother's accordingly, but for five weeks he heard nothing from or of the inexorable Mary, and was glad to beguile his own 'vexing thoughts' by endeavouring to create in his mind an artificial and factitious interest in our cricket-match—all unimportant as such a trifle must have seemed to a man in love. Poor James, however, is a social and warm-hearted person, not likely to resist a contagious sympathy. As the time for the play advanced, the interest which he had at first affected became genuine and sincere: and he was really, when he left the ground on Sunday night, almost as enthusiastically absorbed in the event of the next day, as Joel Brent himself. He little foresaw

111

the new and delightful interest which awaited him at home, where, on the moment of his arrival, his sister-in-law and confidante presented him with a billet from the lady of his heart. It had, with the usual delay of letters sent by private hands in that rank of life, loitered on the road, in a degree inconceivable to those who are accustomed to the punctual speed of the post, and had taken ten days for its twelve miles' journey. Have my readers any wish to see this *billet-doux*? I can show them (but in strict confidence) a literal copy. It was addressed,

> For mistur jem browne
> 'blaxmith by
> 'S'.

The inside ran thus:

'Mistur browne this is to Inform you that oure parish plays bramley men next mondy is a week, i think we shall lose without yew, from your humbell servant to command
'Mary Allen.'

Was there ever a prettier relenting? a summons more flattering, more delicate, more irresistible? The precious epistle was undated; but, having ascertained who brought it, and found, by cross-examining the messenger, that the Monday in question was the very next day, we were not surprised to find that Mistur browne forgot his engagement to us, forgot all but Mary and Mary's letter, and set off at four o'clock the next morning to walk twelve miles, and to play for her parish, and in her sight. Really we must not send James Brown to Coventry—must we? Though if, as his sister-in-law tells our damsel Harriet he hopes to do, he should bring the fair Mary home as his bride, he will not greatly care how little we say to him. But he must not be sent to Coventry—True-love forbid!

At last we were all assembled, and marched down to H. common, the appointed ground, which, though in our dominions according to the maps, was the constant practising place of our opponents, and *terra incognita* to us. We found our adversaries on the ground as we expected, for our various delays had hindered us from taking the field so early as we wished; and as soon as we had settled all preliminaries, the match began.

But alas! I have been so long setting my preliminaries, that I have left myself no room for the detail of our victory, and must squeeze the account of our grand achievements into as little compass as Cowley, when he crammed the names of eleven of his mistresses into the narrow space of four eight-syllable lines. *They* began the warfare—those boastful men of B. And what think you, gentle reader, was the amount of their innings? These challengers—the famous eleven—how many did they get? Think! imagine! guess!—You cannot?—Well! —they got twenty-two, or rather, they got twenty; for two of theirs were short notches, and would never have been allowed, only that, seeing what they were made of, we and our umpires were not particular—They should have had twenty more if they had chosen to claim them. Oh, how well we fielded! and how well we bowled! our good play had quite as much to do with their miserable failure as their bad. Samuel Long is a slow bowler, George Simmons a fast one, and the change from Long's lobbing to Simmons's fast balls posed them completed. Poor simpletons! they were always wrong, expecting the slow for the quick, and the quick for the slow. Well, we went in. And what were our innings? Guess again!—guess! A hundred and sixty-nine! in spite of soaking showers, and wretched ground, where the ball would not run a yard, we headed them by a hundred and forty-seven; and then they gave in, as well they might. William Grey pressed them much to try another innings. 'There was so much chance,' as he courteously observed, 'in cricket, that advantageous as our position seemed, we might, very possibly, be overtaken. The B. men had better try.' But they were beaten sulky and would not move—to my great disappointment; I wanted to prolong the pleasure of success. What a glorious sensation it is to be for five hours together—winning—winning! always feeling what a whist-player feels when he takes up four honours, seven trumps!

Who would think that a little bit of leather and two pieces of wood, had such a delightful and delighting power!

The only drawback on my enjoyment was the failure of the pretty boy, David Willis, who, injudiciously put in first, and playing for the first time in a match amongst men and strangers, who talked to him, and stared at him, was seized with such a fit of shamefaced shyness, that he could scarcely hold his bat, and was bowled out without a stroke, from actual nervousness. 'He will come off that,' Tom Coper says—I am afraid he will. I wonder whether Tom had ever any modesty to lose. Our other modest lad, John Strong, did very well; his length told in fielding and he got good fame. He ran out his mate, Samuel Long; who, I do believe, but for the excess of Joel's eagerness, would have stayed in till this time, by which exploit he got into sad disgrace; and then he himself got thirty-seven runs, which redeemed his reputation. William Grey made a hit which actually lost the cricket-ball. We think she lodged in a hedge, a quarter of a mile off, but nobody could find her. And George Simmons had nearly lost his shoe, which he tossed away in a passion, for having been caught out, owing to the ball glancing against it. These, together with a very complete somerset of Ben Appleton, our long-stop, who floundered about in the mud, making faces and attitudes as laughable as Grimaldi, none could tell whether by accident or design, were the chief incidents of the scene of action. Amongst the spectators nothing remarkable occurred, beyond the general calamity of two or three drenchings, except that a form, placed by the side of a hedge, under a very insufficient shelter, was knocked into the ditch in a sudden rush of the cricketers to escape a pelting shower, by which means all parties shared the fate of Ben Appleton, some on land and some by water; and that, amidst the scramble, a saucy gipsy of a girl contrived to steal from the knee of the demure and well-apparelled Samuel Long, a smart handkerchief which his careful dame had tied round it to preserve his new (what is the mincing feminine word?)— his new—inexpressibles, thus reversing the story of Desdemona, and causing the new Othello to call aloud for his handkerchief, to the great diversion of the company. And so we parted; the players retired to their supper, and we to our homes; all wet through, all good-humoured and happy—except the losers.

Today we are happy too. Hats, with ribands in them, go glancing up and down; and William Grey says, with a proud humility, 'We do not challenge any parish; but if we be challenged we are ready.'

from OUR VILLAGE 1832

IO   *Chrystal's Century*

E. W. HORNUNG

IT REALLY began in the pavilion up at Lord's, since it was off Tuthill that most of the runs were made, and during an Eton and Harrow match that the little parson begged him to play. They had been in the same Harrow eleven some eighteen years before. The Reverend Gerald Osborne had afterwards touched the hem of first-class cricket, while Tuthill, who captained a minor county, was still the very finest second-class bowler in England.

'Who's it against?' asked Tuthill, with a suspicious glint in his clear eye; for if he was not good enough for first-class cricket, third-class was not good enough for him.

'A man who's made his pile and bought himself a place near Elstree; they let him have a week in August on the school ground, and I ran the side against him for the last match.'

'Decent wicket, then,' said Tuthill, with a critical eye upon the Eton bowling.

'I shouldn't wonder if you found it a bit fiery,' said the crafty priest, with a timely memory of Tuthill's happiest hunting-ground. 'And they'll put you up and do you like a Coronation guest.'

'I don't care twopence about that,' said Tuthill. 'Will they keep my analysis?'

'I'll guarantee it, Tuttles,' said the little parson.

And Tuttles consulted the diary of a conscientious cricketer.

'I can,' said he, 'and I don't see why I shouldn't. I was coming up for the Oval Test in any case. It will only mean taking another day or two while I am about it. You can put me down.'

'And rely on you?' added the other, as one whose fortune was too good to be true.

'My dear Jerry,' cried Tuttles, with characteristic emphasis, 'I never chucked a match in all my life! It's a promise, and I'll be there if no one else is. But who is this sporting pal of yours? I suppose he has a name?'

Osborne went out of his way to applaud a somewhat inferior stroke by the Harrow boy who was making all the runs.

'As a matter of fact,' he finally confessed, 'he was at school with us, though you probably don't remember him. His name's Chrystal.'

'Not old Ginger Chrystal, surely?'

'I believe they did call him Ginger. I don't remember him at school.'

'But I do! He was in our house, and super'd, poor beast! Ginger Chrystal! Why on earth didn't you tell me who it was before?'

'You've named one of my reasons, Tuttles. He's a bit shy about his Harrow days. Then he says himself that he was no more use at cricket than he was at work, and I thought it might put you off.'

'No more he was,' said Tuttles reflectively. 'Do you mean to say he's any good now?'

'No earthly,' replied the little parson, with his cherub's smile; 'only just about the keenest rabbit in the whole cricket warren!'

The finest second-class bowler in England displayed a readiness of appreciation doubly refreshing in an obviously critical temperament.

'And yet you say he has done himself well!' he added incredulously, as his mirth subsided.

'Only made a hundred thousand in South America, Tuttles.'

'Nonsense!'

'It might be double by the way he does things.'

'That utter rabbit at every mortal thing?'

'He's not one now, Tuttles, at anything but cricket. That's his only weak point. At everything else Chrystal's one of the smartest chaps you ever met, though he does weigh you and me put together, and quite one of the best. But he's so mad-keen on cricket that he keeps a pro. for himself and his son of seven, and by practising more than any man in England he scores his ten runs in all matches every season. However, when this boy runs into three figures, or gets out, you must come and meet the modern Chrystal in the flesh; there's plenty of it, though not too much for the heart inside, and at the present moment he's spreading every ounce of himself in a coach he's got here in my name.'

It was a fair enough picture that the parson drew, for Chrystal was really corpulent, though tall and finely built. He wore a stubby moustache of the hue which had earned him his school nickname, but underneath were the mouth of a strong man and the smile of a sweet woman. It was a beaming, honest unassuming face; but the womanly quality reappeared in a pair of very shapely, well-kept hands, one of which could come down with virile force on Tuthill's shoulder, while the other injured the most cunning bunch of fingers in second-class cricket. Then a shyness overcame the great fellow, and the others all saw that he was thinking of the one inglorious stage of his career. And his wife, a beautiful woman, took charge of little Osborne; and Tuthill, who had sense and tact, congratulated Chrystal point-blank and at once upon his great success in life.

But for an instant Chrystal looked quite depressed, as though success at school was the only sort worth achieving; then his smile came out like the sun, and his big body began to shake.

'Yes,' he whispered, 'they promised me a dog's life and a felon's death because I couldn't make Latin verses! Do you remember my second half of a pentameter?'

'Laomedontiaden!' cried Tuthill, convulsed with laughter at the sudden reminiscence.

'I never could see where the laugh came in,' confessed Chrystal, like the man he was. 'But I've no doubt that was what cooked my goose.'

Tuthill was much impressed.

'And he never said it didn't matter,' as he afterwards put it to the parson, 'or changed the subject to the things he has done, or took out a big gold watch, or drowned us in champagne, or did or said a single thing that wouldn't have done honour to the bluest blood on the ground. All he did say, at the end of the innings, was that he'd give half he'd got to have been in the eleven himself! Oh, yes, I've promised to play in his all right; who could refuse a chap like that? I'm going for the whole week; let's only hope he won't drop all his catches off my stuff.'

'You must forgive him his trespasses, Tuttles,' the clergyman said, with some gravity, and no irreverence at all.

'I can't forgive that one,' replied the candid demon of second-class cricket. 'I never could, and never shall.'

But it was not for Tuthill to forgive when the great week came, or at all events, before the week was at an end. It is true that the catches followed the non-cricketer to every position in the field, as catches will, and equally true that a large majority of them were duly 'put on the floor'. But, as good luck and his own accuracy would have it, the great bowler was not usually the sufferer. Once, indeed, when it was otherwise, he did tell his host, with unpremeditated emphasis, that the ball wouldn't bite him; but that was the only contretemps of the kind, and an ample apology followed when the wicket fell. But a more ample revenge was in store for the moving spirit of the week.

It had gone like wedding-bells from the first over of the first match; even the most hardened country-house cricketer of the party could not look back upon a better time. Mrs Chrystal proved a charming hostess, and Chrystal a 'heavenly host' according to one of the many mushroom humorists who shot up in the genial atmosphere of his house. The house itself was old and red and mellow, but none the worse for the electric light and the porcelain baths which Chrystal had put in. The place, like so many in that neighbourhood was a mass of roses, and a stroll in the garden after dinner was like swimming in scent. There was a waggonette to take the players to the ground, a daily sweepstake on the highest scorer, a billiard handicap for the evenings. Creature comforts were provided on a scale which fell deliberately short of plutocratic display, but of no other standard applicable to the case. Finally, the weather was such as an English summer can still produce in penitent mood; and the only cloud of any sort that brooded over the week was the secret cloud in Robert Chrystal's heart; for it was half-broken by a sequence of failure most abject even for him.

'Four runs all the week, and they were an overthrow,' said he, with a rueful humour which but partially disguised the tremendous tragedy of the thing. 'Three times first ball! I'll tell you what I'll do before next August: I'll lay out a ground of my own, and it shall have a subterranean passage from the wicket to the pavilion. Either that, or let me be translated like Enoch when it happens to me again!'

There was one who whispered that it would be the first translation he had ever achieved; but even that wag would have made Chrystal a present of his highest score, and they all felt the same. None more sympathetic than Tuttles when it was merely a batting misfortune; up to the Friday night he had twenty-nine for two hundred and thirty-one, and but for Chrystal it would have been twenty-eight for two hundred and thirty. Little Jerry Osborne was also full of sympathy, though he expressed it rather often, and gave Chrystal more advice than he was likely to have the least opportunity of following. One excellent fellow happened to have played in a match, some seasons before, in which Chrystal had actually made runs; and he talked about that. He reminded Chrystal of it every day. 'They were all from the middle of the bat. The man who took thirty-six like that may take a century any day. You've struck a bad patch, as we all do, and you've lost confidence; you shouldn't take it so seriously.' A tall Quidnunc, who said little but made his hundred most days, did declare after Chrystal's congratulations (in the hour of his own disaster) upon one of them, that he was 'Absolutely the best sportsman in Europe'; the grave Indian major treated him with silent respect; and the young schoolmasters, who made up the team and did the deep-field business, agreed most piously with the Quidnunc.

The poor devil was a cricketer at the core. That was the hard part. And he knew the game as many a real cricketer does not; you never heard Chrystal disparage the ball that had just bowled him; neither was it ever 'a ball that might have beaten Charles Fry.' He always knew, none better, exactly what he had done, and (which was more galling) precisely what he ought to have done. If he had made a half-volley into a yorker, he was the first to tell you so. He knew when he had played across a plain straight one, when he had failed to swing his left foot far enough over, or played at the pitch of a long-hop. Even as the wicket rattled he was playing the stroke again, and with academic correctness, in his own mind. That was Chrystal's cricket. Then he would walk back swinging his glove, and beginning to smile when the maker of centuries begins to run— to smile all over a face that felt like a death's head. And that was the stuff of which the man was made.

It was the Friday night, and all the others were so pleased

122

with themselves! Everybody else had at least one little achievement of his own to form a gratifying reflection, and to justify
his place in the team. Chrystal could hear them in the billiard
room, and at the piano, as for a few minutes he walked up and
down outside, with the wife from whom even he could not
conceal his consuming chagrin.

'They're in great spirits!' Chrystal had exclaimed, with no
bitterness in his voice, but with a whole tome of mortification.
And his wife had pressed his arm; she had not made the
mistake of going on to remind him that cricket was only a
game, and that he could afford to fail at games.

'I believe you'll do better tomorrow,' was what she did say,
with a quiet conviction not unjustified by the doctrine of
chances in the mind of a lady who declined to regard cricket
as a game of skill.

'Tomorrow!' Chrystal laughed outright. 'Why, if one could
score a minus, that's what I should make tomorrow!'

'Is there any special reason for saying that?'

'There is,' said Chrystal grimly. 'There's good old Tuttles
against us, for a change. He'll bowl me neck and crop first
ball!'

They took another turn in silence.

'I'm not sure,' said Mrs Chrystal, 'that I quite like Mr Tuttles.'

'Not like old Tuttles? Why on earth not?'

'He has such a good opinion of himself.'

'He has reason!' cried Chrystal, with hardly ten per cent of
envy in his loyal tone.

'Then I do think he's rather spiteful. To go and bowl you out
first ball—if he did.'

'He'd bowl me out if I was his long-lost brother! He's so
keen; and quite right, too. You've got to play the game, dear.'

If it had been the game of battle, murder, and sudden death,
Chrystal's manner could not possibly have been more serious.

But a silence had fallen on piano and billiard-table; and
Chrystal hurried indoors, as he said, 'to keep the ball rolling if I
can't hit it.' They were only talking about the final match, how-

123

ever, in which Chrystal played his gardeners and grooms while little Osborne took the field against him with the like raw material from his own parish near Ware.

'It's all very well,' said Chrystal, joining in the cricket talk that was beginning to get on his nerves; 'but I ought really to object to Tuttles, you know. He has neither the birth qualification nor the residential; he isn't even your deputy-assistant-secretary, Jerry!'

'I suppose you really don't object?' said Tuttles himself, in the nicest way, the first time he and Chrystal were more or less alone.

'My dear fellow!' was all Chrystal said in reply. 'I want to see you take all the wickets,' he added; 'I promise you mine.'

Tuthill smiled at the superfluous concession.

'I'll have to do my best,' said he, as the hangman might of his painful duty. 'But, as a matter of fact, I'm not sure that my best will amount to much tomorrow. I've been bowling a bit too much, and a bit too well. My off day's about due, and on my off day I'm a penny treat. Full-pitches to leg and long-hops into the slips!'

Chrystal's mouth watered! The second sort of ball was often fatal to him, but the first was the one delivery with which he was almost as much at home in practice as in theory. He had seldom run into double figures without the aid of the repeated full-pitch to leg.

It so happened that there was rain in the night, but only enough to improve a pitch which had quite fulfilled little Osborne's promise of fire; and an absence of sun next day averted an even more insidious state of things. The last match was thus played on the worst day and the best wicket of the week. The ball came along stump-high without any tricks at all. Yet Osborne's side was out shortly after lunch for something under a hundred runs, of which Osborne himself made more than half. Tuthill, who did not take his batting seriously, but hit hard and clean as long as he was there, was beginning to look as though he never need get out when Chrystal, of all

124

people, held him low down at point. It was a noble effort in a stout, slow man, but Tuthill walked away without a word. He was keen enough on his innings as long as he was in; but at luncheon he was the first to compliment Chrystal, who had not been so happy all that week. Chrystal had written himself last in the order, but, thus encouraged, he was persuaded to give himself one more chance, and finally went in fourth wicket down.

It was then 3.20 by the clock on the little pavilion, and one of those grey, mild days which are neither close nor cold, and far from unpleasant on the cricket field. The four wickets had fallen for less than forty runs, but Tuthill had only one victim, and it really did appear to be his off day; but he looked grim and inexorable enough as he waited by the umpire while Chrystal took centre and noted that it was now 3.21; at 3.22 he would be safe back in the pavilion, and his cricket troubles would be over for the season, if not for his life.

But the first ball was that wide long-hop of which Tuthill himself had spoken; down it skimmed, small as a racket-ball to Chrystal's miserable eye; he felt for it with half his heart, but luckily heard nothing before the dull impact of the ball in the gloves of an agile wicket-keeper standing back.

'No!' cried the tall Quidnunc at the opposite end; and Chrystal began to feel that he was playing an innings.

The second ball was the other infallible sign of Tuthill's off-day; it was a knee-high full-pitch just wide of Chrystal's pads; and he succeeded in flicking it late and fine, so that it skimmed to the boundary at its own pace. For one wretched moment Chrystal watched the umpire, who happened to be the man who had advised him not to take his cricket so seriously, and who now read his anxiety in a flash.

'That was a hit!' the unorthodox official shouted towards the scorers' table.

'And a jolly good one!' added the tall Quidnunc, while more distant applause reached the striker's trembling ears, and the ardent Tuttles waited for the ball with the face of a handsome

125

fiend. Yet his next was nothing deadlier than a slow half-volley outside the off-stump, which Chrystal played gently but firmly as a delicate stroke at billiards, but with the air of Greek meeting Greek. Already the ball was growing larger and the time was 3.25.

Osborne was bowling at the other end; he always was either batting, bowling, or keeping wicket; but the bowler's was the only department of the game at which he exposed a definite inferiority. He was, however, very fond of bowling, and as he could claim two of the four wickets which had already fallen (one having been run out) it was extremely unlikely that he would spare himself until the tenth one fell. Osborne's first over after Chrystal's arrival was one of his least expensive. The Quid drove him for a languid single while Chrystal, after keeping out of mischief for four balls, sent the fifth high and dry through the slips for three. The stroke was a possible chance to none other than Tuthill, but it was not off his own bowling, and the impression upon the observant spectator must have been a bad one.

'Don't begin by running yourself off your legs,' Chrystal's partner crossed over to advise him between the overs. 'There's the whole afternoon before us, and you won't have many to run for me. I'm as limp as a wet rag, and my only chance of staying here is to sit on the splice while you punch 'em. But don't you be in any hurry; play yourself in.'

If Chrystal had made a respectable score every day, the tone of the best batsman on the side could not have betrayed more confidence in him; he began to feel confidence; the ball swelled to its normal size, and Tuttles' next long-hop went to third man for another sharp single. Chrystal apologized, but his partner had called him in response to an appealing look; evidently he was not too limp to run his captain's hits; it was only Chrystal himself who puffed and blew and leant upon his bat.

And even by the half-hour he was within a run of that two-figure rubicon which he had not passed for two seasons; his face showed the pale determination of a grave endeavour; in fact, it would hurt him more to get out now than to fall as usual to his only ball.

Yet what did happen? It was Tuthill's slow yorker, and Chrystal was in many minds from the time it left the bowler's hand; his good blade wagged irresolutely and the odious projectile was under it in a twinkling. But at the instant the umpire threw up his arm with a yell, and Chrystal never heard the havoc behind him; he was only instinctively aware of it as he watched Tuthill turn upon a comrade who had donned the long white coat over his flannels.

'No *what*?' demanded the best bowler in second-class cricket. 'I said "no ball"!'

'You're the first man who ever said it to me in my life,' remarked Tuttles, deadly calm, while he looked the other up and down as a new species of cricket curiosity. Then he held up his hands for the ball. 'There's a man still in,' he cried; and proceeded to send down a perfectly vicious full-pitcher upon Chrystal's legs, which the captain, who had the single virtue of never running away, promptly despatched for another four.

He had now made thirteen runs in less than thirteen minutes, and already the whole world was a different place, and that part of it a part of Paradise. He was emboldened to glance towards the seats: there was his dear wife strolling restlessly with her parasol, and their tiny boy clapping his hands. Chrystal could see how excited they were at a hundred yards; it only had the effect of making him perversely calm. 'I'm all right—I've got going at last!' he felt tempted to sing out to them; for he felt all right. He had even passed the stage of anticipating the imminent delivery and playing at the ball he expected instead of at the ball that came along. This had been one of Chrystal's many methods of getting rid of himself in the first over. And he had more suicidal strokes than an Indian Prince has scoring ones. But now he looked from his family in the long-field to the noble trees to square-leg, and from the trees down-hill to the reservoir gleaming through third-man's legs; it was hardly credible that he had wished to drown himself in its depths both yesterday and the day before.

The worst player in the world, with his eye in, may resist indefinitely the attack of the best bowler; after all, a ball is a ball and a bat is a bat; and if you once begin getting the one continually in the middle of the other, and keeping it out of harm's way, there is no more to be said and but little to be done. Chrystal was soon meeting every ball in the middle of a bat which responded to the unparalleled experience by driving deliciously. The majority of his strokes were not ideal, though even a critical Cambridge Quid was able to add a stimulating 'good shot!' to not a few, while some were really quite hard and clean. Never before had this batsman felt the bat leap in his hands, and the ball spring from the blade beyond the confines of his wildest hopes, at an unimagined velocity, half so often as he experienced these great sensations now. Great! What is there in the sensual world to put on the same page with them? And let your real batsman bear in mind that these divine moments, and their blessed memory, are greatest of all where they are most rare; in his heart who never had the makings of a real batsman, but who once in his life had played a decent game.

Chrystal was in heaven. No small boy succeeding in his first little match, no international paragon compiling his cool hundred before fifty thousand eyes, was ever granted the joy of the game in fuller or sweeter or more delirious measure than was Robert Chrystal that afternoon. Think of his failures. Think of his years. Think of his unathletic figure. Think of ball after ball—big as a football to him now—yet diminishing into thin air or down the hill or under the trees. 'Thank God there's a boundary!' murmured Chrystal, wiping his face while they fetched it. Yet he was cool enough in the way that mattered. He had lost all thought of his score. His mind was entirely concentrated on the coming ball; but it was an open mind until the ball arrived. If his thoughts wandered between the overs, it was back to Harrow, and to the pleasing persuasion that he might have been in the eleven but for his infernal ineptitude for

Latin verses. Meanwhile, every ball brought its own anxiety and delight. And for several overs there was really very little to criticize except his style; then came an awful moment.

It was a half-volley on his legs, and Chrystal hit it even higher than he intended, but not quite so hard. One of those vigorous young schoolmasters was keeping himself hard and fit at deep mid-on; he had to run like a greyhound, and to judge a cross flight as he ran; but the apparent impossibility of the catch was simply a challenge to the young schoolmaster's calibre as a field; the ground was just covered, and the ball just held with extended hand. It was a supreme effort—or would have been. There are those catches which are held almost, but not quite, long enough to count. This was an exaggerated instance. Unable to check himself, the young schoolmaster must have covered at least a yard with the ball in his hand. Then it rolled out, and he even kicked it far in front of him in his headlong stride.

'Got him! No, he hasn't. Put him on the floor!' Chrystal heard the little parson say, as he himself charged down the pitch in his second run. He saw nothing. His partner was calling him for a third, and Tuttles was stamping and raving at the bowler's end.

'Was that a chance?' gasped Chrystal, as he grounded his bat.

'A chance?' snorted Tuttles. 'My dear fellow, he only held it about twenty minutes!'

'Am I out, then?' asked Chrystal of the umpire, his hot blood running cold.

'Not out!' declared that friendly functionary without an instant's indecision. 'But I wouldn't appeal against myself, old chap! It's sporting, but it isn't war.'

The incident, however, had a disturbing effect upon Chrystal's nerves. He shuddered to think of his escape. He became self-conscious, and began to think about his score. It was quite a long time since they clapped him for his fifty. He must be in the eighties at the very least. On his own ground he would have the public scoring apparatus that they have at

Lord's; then you would always know when you were near your century. Chrystal, however, was well aware that he must be pretty near his. He had hit another four, not one of his best, and given a stumping chance to little Osborne, who had more than once exchanged the ball for the gloves during the past two hours.

Yes, it was a quarter past five. Chrystal saw that, and pulled himself together, for his passive experience of the game reminded him that the average century is scored in a couple of hours. No doubt he must be somewhere about the nineties. Everybody seemed very still in the pavilion. The scorers' table was certainly surrounded. Chrystal set his teeth, and smothered a half-volley in his earlier no-you-don't manner. But the next ball could only have bowled him round his legs, and Tuttles hardly ever broke that way, besides which, this one was too fast, and, in short, away it went skimming towards the trees. And there and then arose the sweetest uproar that Robert Chrystal had ever heard in all his life.

They were shouting themselves hoarse in front of the little pavilion. The group about the scoring table was dispersing with much hat-waving. The scorer might have been seen leaning back in his chair like a man who had been given air at last. Mrs Chrystal was embracing the boy, probably (and in fact) to hide her joyous tears. Chrystal himself felt almost overcome, and quite abashed. Should he take his cap off or should he not? He would know better another time; meanwhile he meant to look modest, and did look depressed; and half the field closed in upon him, clapping their unselfish hands, while a pair of wicket-keeping gloves belaboured his back with ostentatious thuds.

More magnanimous than the rest, Tuttles had been the first to clap, but he was also the first to stop clapping, and there was a business air about the way in which he signalled for the ball. He carried it back to the spot where he started his run with as much deliberation as though measuring the distance for an opening over. There was peculiar care also in the way in which he grasped the leather, rolling it affectionately in his hand, as though wiping off the sawdust which it had not been necessary to use since the morning. There was a grim light in his eye as he stood waiting to begin his run, a subtle something in the run itself, the whole reminding one, with a sudden and characteristic emphasis, that this really was the first bowler in second-class cricket. A few quick steps firm and precise; a couple of long ones, a beautiful swing, a lovely length, and Chrystal's middle stump lay stretched upon the grass.

It was a great ending to a great innings, a magnificent finale to a week of weeks; but on the charming excesses on the field I shall touch no more than on the inevitable speeches that night at dinner. Field and house alike were full of good hearts, of hearts good enough to appreciate a still better one. Tuthill's was the least expansive; but he had the critical temperament, and he had been hit for many fours, and his week's analysis had been ruined in an afternoon.

'I wasn't worth a sick headache,' he told Chrystal himself, with his own delightful mixture of frankness and contempt, 'I couldn't have outed the biggest sitter in Christendom.'

'But you did send down some pretty good ones, you know!' replied Chrystal, with a rather wistful intonation.

'A few,' Tuttles allowed charily. 'The one that bowled you was all right. But it was a very good innings, and I congratulate you again.'

Now Chrystal had some marvellous old brandy; how it had come into his possession, and how much it was worth, were, respectively, a very long and rather a tall story. He only broached a bottle upon very great occasions; but this was obviously one, even though the bottle had been the last in the cellar, and its contents liquid gold. The only question was whether they should have it on the table with dessert or with their coffee in the study.

Chrystal debated the point with some verbosity; the fact was that he had been put to shame by hearing and speaking of nothing but his century from the soup to the speeches; and he resolutely introduced and conscientiously enlarged upon the topic of the brandy in order to throw a deliberate haze over his own lustre. His character shone the more brilliantly through it; but that could be said of each successive incident since his great achievement. He beamed more than ever. In a sudden silence you would have expected to catch him purring. And Mrs Chrystal had at last agreed to his giving her those particular diamonds which she had over and over again dissuaded him from buying: if he must make some offering to his earthly gods it might as well be to the goddess on the hearth. But none of themselves knew of this, and it was of the Chrystal known to men as well that all sat talking when he had left the dining-room with his bunch of keys. Mrs Chrystal felt the tears coming back into her eyes; they were every one so fond of him, and yet he was all and only hers! It was she who made the move, and for this reason, though she said she fancied he must be expecting them to follow him to the study, for he had been several minutes gone. But Mrs Chrystal led the other ladies to the drawing-room, merely pausing to say generally to the men:

'If you don't find him there he must have gone to the cellar himself, and I'm afraid he's having a hunt.'

Now the Chrystals, like a sensible couple, never meddled with each other's definite departments in the house, and of course Mrs Chrystal knew no more about her husband's cellar arrangements than he did of the inside of her store-room. Otherwise she would have known that he very seldom entered his own cellar, and that he did not require to go there for his precious brandy.

Yet he did seem to have gone there now, for there was no sign of him in the study when the cricketers trooped in. Osborne was saying something in a lowered voice to Tuthill, who, looking round the empty room, replied as emphatically as usual.

'I'm glad you think I did it well. Man and boy, I never took on such a job in all my days, and I never will another. The old sitter!'

132

And he chuckled good-humouredly enough.

'It's all right, he's down in the cellar,' the little clergyman explained. 'Trust us not to give the show away.'

'And me,' nodded the scholastic hero of the all-but-gallery-catch.

'You precious near did!' Osborne remonstrated. 'You held it just two seconds too long.'

'But fancy holding it at all! I never thought I could get near the thing. I thought a bit of a dash would contribute to the general verisimilitude. Then to make the catch of a lifetime and to have to drop it like a hot potato!'

'It showed the promising quality of self-restraint,' the clerical humorist allowed. 'You will be an upper usher yet.'

'Or a husher upper?' suggested a wag of baser mould, to wit, the sympathetic umpire of the afternoon. 'But your side-show wasn't a patch on mine. Even Osborne admits that you had two seconds to think about it. I hadn't the fifth of one. Tuttles, old man, I thought you were going to knock me down!'

'I very nearly did,' the candid bowler owned. 'I never was no-balled in my life before, and for the moment I forgot.'

'Then it wasn't all acting?'

'Half and half.'

'I thought it was too good to be untrue.'

'But,' continued Tuttles with his virile vanity, 'you fellows buck about what you did, as though you'd done, between you, a thousandth part of what I did. You had your moment apiece. I had one every ball of every over. Great Lord! if I'd known how hard it would be to bowl tosh. Full-pitches on the pads! that's a nice length to have to live up to through a summer afternoon. I wouldn't do it again for five-and-twenty golden sovereigns!'

'And I,' put in the quiet Quidnunc. 'It's the first time I ever sat on the splice while the other man punched them, and I hope it's the last.'

He had been tried as a bat for an exceptionally strong Cambridge eleven.

'Come, come,' said the grave major. 'I wasn't in this myself. I distinctly disapproved. But he played quite well when he got his eye in. I don't believe you could have bowled him then if you'd tried.'

'My good sir,' said he, 'what about the ball after the one which ran him into three figures?'

'Where *is* the dear old rabbit?' the ex-umpire exclaimed.

'Well, not in the hutch,' said the little parson. 'He's come right out of that, and I shouldn't be surprised if he stopped out. I only wish it was the beginning of the week.'

'I'm going to look for him,' the other rejoined, with the blank eye that has not seen a point. He stepped through a French window out into the night. The young schoolmasters followed him. The Indian major detained Osborne.

'We ought to make a rule not to speak of this again. It would be too horrible if it leaked out!'

'I suppose it would.' The little parson had become more like one. Though full of cricket and of chaff, and gifted with a peculiarly lay vocabulary for the due ventilation of his favourite topic, he was yet no discredit to the cloth. A certain superficial insincerity was his worst fault; the conspiracy, indeed, had originated in his nimble mind; but its execution had far exceeded his conception. On the deeper issues the man was sound.

'Can there be any doubt?' the major pursued.

'About the momentary bitter disappointment, no, I'm afraid not; about the ultimate good all round no again; but there I don't fear, I hope.'

'I don't quite follow you,' said the major.

'Old Bob Chrystal,' continued Osborne, 'is absolutely the best sportsman in the world, and absolutely the dearest good chap. But until this afternoon I never thought he would get within a hundred miles of decent cricket; and now I almost think he might, even at his age. He has had the best practice he ever had in his life. His shots improved as he went on. You saw for yourself how he put on the wood. It is a liberal cricket education to make runs, even against the worst bowling in the world. Like most other feats, once you get going, every ten runs come easier than the last. Chrystal got a hundred this afternoon because we let him. I said just now I wished it was the beginning of the week. Don't you see my point?'

The major looked a brighter man.

'You think he might get another?'

'I don't mind betting he does,' said the little parson, 'if he sticks to the country cricket long enough. *Possunt quia posse videntur*!'

They went out in their turn; and Chrystal himself at last stole forth from the deep cupboard in which he kept his cigars and his priceless brandy. An aged bottle still trembled in his hand; but a little while ago his lip had been trembling also, and now it was not. Of course he had not understood a word of the little clergyman's classical tag; but all that immediately preceded it had made, or may make, nearly all the difference to the rest of even his successful life.

His character had been in the balance during much of what had passed in his hearing, and yet behind his back; whether it would have emerged triumphant, even without Gerald Osborne's final pronouncement, is for others to judge from what they have seen of it in this little record.

'It was most awfully awkward,' so Chrystal told his wife. 'I was in there getting at the brandy—I'd gone and crowded it up with all sorts of tackle—when you let all those fellows into the study, and they began talking about me before I could give the alarm. Then it was too late. It would have made them so uncomfortable, and I should have looked so mean.'

'I hope they were saying nice things?'

'Oh, rather; but don't you let them know I overheard them, mind.'

Mrs Chrystal seemed the least suspicious.

'About your century, darling?'

'Well, partly. It was little Osborne, you know. He knows more about cricket than any of them. Tuttles is only a bowler.'

'I *don't* like him,' said Mrs Chrystal. 'I've quite made up my mind. He was trying to bowl you out the whole time.'

'Little Osborne,' her husband continued, rather hastily, 'says I ought to make a hundred—another hundred—if I stick to it.'

'But of course you will,' said Mrs Chrystal, who just then would have taken Chrystal's selection for England as a matter of course.

Her husband was blushing a little, but glowing more. It was one of those moments when you would have understood his making so much money and winning such. Never was a mouth so determined, and yet so good.

'I don't know about that, dear,' he opened it to say, 'but I mean to try!'

I I *Tom Richardson*

SIR NEVILLE CARDUS

ON JUNE 26, 1902, Old Trafford was a place of Ethiopic heat, and the crowd that sat there in an airless world saw J. T. Tyldesley flog the Surrey bowlers all over the field. Richardson attacked from the Stretford end, and at every over's finish he wiped the sweat from his brow and felt his heart beating hammer strokes. Richardson had all his fieldsmen on the off side, save one, who 'looked out' at mid-on. And once (and once only) he bowled a long hop to Tyldesley, who swung on his heels and hooked the ball high and far into the on field. The Surrey fieldsman at mid wicket saw something pass him, and with his eye helplessly followed the direction of the hit. 'One boundary more or less don't count on a day like this,' it was possible to imagine the sweltering fellow telling himself. 'Besides, Johnny's plainly going to get 'em anyhow.' The ball slackened pace on the boundary's edge. Would it just roll home? The crowd tried to cheer it to the edge of the field. Then one was aware of heavy thuds on the earth. Some Surrey man, after all, had been fool enough to think a desperate spurt and a boundary saved might be worth while, blistering sun despite. Who on earth was the stout but misguided sportsman? Heaven be praised, it was Richardson himself. He had bowled the ball; he had been bowling balls, and his fastest, for nearly two hours. His labours in the sun had made ill those who sat watching him. And here he was, pounding along the outfield, after a hit from his own bowling. The writer sat on the 'popular' side, under the score-board, as the ball got home a foot in advance of Richardson. The impetus of his run swept him over the edge of the grass, and to stop himself he put out his arms and grasped the iron rail. He laughed—the handsomest laugh in the world—and said 'Thank you' to somebody who

137

threw the ball back to him. His face was wet, his breath scant. He was the picture of honest toil. With the ball in his hands again he trotted back to the wicket and once more went through the travail of bowling at J. T. Tyldesley on a pitiless summer's day.

This was Tom Richardson all over—the cricketer whose heart was so big that even his large body hardly contained its heroic energy. And this hot June morning the crowd mused about a day that had dragged out an intolerable length six years earlier—in 1896—on which England had struggled bitterly with Australia at Old Trafford, and Tom Richardson had touched as sublime a heroism as ever cricketer knew. This Manchester Test match of July, 1896, seems now to have been fought on so vast a scale that it might well be thought none but giants could have sustained the burden of it. Yet when Richardson's part in it is retold he was a very colossus that made pigmies of the others—made even Ranji a pigmy, despite that he played the innings of his life.

Australia batted first and scored 412. England—with Grace, Ranji, Stoddart, Abel, Jackson, J. T. Brown, MacLaren, Lilley, and Briggs to look to for runs—were all out for 231, and the Australian captain sent us in again. And once more the English cracks were reduced to littleness—all save Ranji, who, in Giffen's term, 'conjured' an innings of 154 not out, out of the total of 305. Australia needed 125 for victory—a mere song on the wicket. Old Trafford gave itself up to the doldrums as soon as Iredale and Trott had comfortably made a score or so without loss. Then it was that Richardson's face was seen to be grim—his customary happy smile gone. In Australia's first innings he had bowled 68 overs for seven wickets and 168 runs. Yet he was here again, bowling like a man just born to immortal energy. And four Australian wickets were down for 45 in an hour. If only England had given the Australians a few more runs, the crowd wished out of its heart—if only Richardson could keep up his pace for another hour. But, of course, no man could expect him to bowl in this superhuman

138

vein for long. . . . Thus did the crowd sigh and regret. But Richardson's spirit *did* go on burning a dazzling flame. The afternoon moved slowly to the sunset—every hour an eternity. And Richardson *did* bowl and bowl and bowl, and his fury diminished not a jot. Other English bowlers faltered, but not Richardson. The fifth Australian wicket fell at 79, the sixth at 95, the seventh at 100. The Australians now wanted 25, with only three wickets in keeping. McKibbin and Jones—two rabbits—amongst them. 'Is it possible?' whispered the crowd. 'Can it be? Can we win . . . after all? . . .' Why, look at Richardson and see: England must win. This man is going to suffer no frustration. He has bowled for two hours and a half, without a pause. He has bowled till Nature has pricked him with protesting pains in every nerve, in every muscle of his great frame. He has bowled till Nature can no longer make him aware that she is abused outrageously, for now he is a man in a trance, the body of him numbed and moving automatically to the only suggestion his consciousness can respond to—'England must win, must win, must win.' . . . With nine runs still to be got by Australia, Kelly gave a chance to Lilley at the wicket and Lilley let the ball drop to the earth. The heart of Richardson might have burst at this, but it did not. To the end he strove and suffered.

Australia won by three wickets, and the players ran from the field—all of them save Richardson. He stood at the bowling crease, dazed. *Could* the match have been lost? his spirit protested. Could it be that the gods had looked on and permitted so much painful striving to go by unrewarded? His body still shook from the violent motion. He stood there like some fine animal baffled at the uselessness of great strength and effort in this world. . . . A companion led him to the pavilion, and there he fell wearily to a seat. That afternoon Richardson had laboured for three mortal hours without rest. In the match he bowled 110 overs and three balls, for 13 wickets and 244 runs. He never bowled again in a Test match at Manchester.

This man Richardson was the greatest cricketer that ever

took to fast bowling. Lockwood had nicer technical shades than Richardson—a guile which was alien to the honest heart of Richardson. But Lockwood had not a great spirit. He was a bowler at the mercy of a mood; an artist with an artist's capriciousness. Richardson bowled from a natural impulse to bowl, and whether he bowled well or ill that impulse was always strong. His action moved one like music because it was so rhythmical. He ran to the wicket a long distance, and at the bowling crease his terminating leap made you catch breath. His break-back most cricketers of his day counted among the seven wonders of the game. He could pitch a ball outside the wicket on the hardest turf and hit the leg stump. The break was, of course, an action break; at the moment of 'release' his fingers swept across the ball and the body was flung towards the left. And his length was as true as Attewell's own. But who is going to talk of Richardson's art in terms of the 'filthily technical,' as Mr Kipling would call it? His bowling was wonderful because into it went the very life-force of the man—the triumphant energy that made him in his hey-day seem one of Nature's announcements of the joy of life. It was sad to see Richardson grow old, to see the fires in him burn low. Cricketers like Richardson ought never to know of old age. Every springtime ought to find them newborn, like the green world they live in.

12   *Glimpses of Hambledon*

JOHN NYREN

NO ELEVEN in England could compare with the Hambledon which met on the first Tuesday in May on Broad-Halfpenny. So renowned a set were these men that the whole county round would flock to see one of their trial matches. During the solemnity of our great matches it was a heart-stirring sight to witness the multitude forming a complete and dense circle round that noble green. Little Hambledon pitted against All England was a proud thought for the Hampshire men. There would this company remain patiently and anxiously watching every turn of fate in the game, as if the event had been the meeting of two armies to decide their liberty. And whenever a Hambledon man made a good hit, worth four or five runs, you would hear the deep mouths of the whole multitude baying away in pure Hampshire—'Go hard!—go hard!—*Tich* and turn!—*tich* and turn!' Grand matches were always made for £500 a side and at a match of the Hambledon Club against All England the club had to go in to get the runs, and there was a long number of them. It became quite apparent that the game would be closely fought. Noah Mann kept worrying old Nyren to let him go in, and although he became quite indignant at his constant refusal, our General knew what he was about in keeping him back. At length, when the last but one was out, he sent Mann in, and there were then ten runs to get. The sensation now all over the ground was greater than anything of the kind I ever witnessed before or since. All knew the state of the game, and many thousands were hanging upon this narrow point. There was Sir Horace Mann, walking about, outside the ground, cutting down the daisies with his stick—a habit with him when he was agitated; the old farmers leaning forward upon their

141

tall old staves, and the whole multitude perfectly still. After Noah had had one or two balls, Lumpy tossed one a little too far, when our fellow got in, and hit it out in his grand style. Six of the ten were gained. Never shall I forget the roar that followed this hit. Then there was a dead stand for some time, and no runs were made; ultimately, however, he gained them all, and won the game. After he was out, he upbraided Nyren for

CRICKET. Played by the Gentlemen's Club. White Conduit House . 1784 .

not putting him in earlier. 'If you had let me go in an hour ago,' said he, 'I would have served them in the same way.' But the old tactician was right for he knew Noah to be a man of such nerve and self-possession, that the thought of so much depending upon him would not have the paralysing effect that it would upon many others. He was sure of him, and Noah afterwards felt the compliment . . .

I remember when upon one occasion Miller and Minshull,

being in together, had gained an uncommon number of runs, the backers of the Hambledon men, Dehaney and Paulet, began to quake, and edged off all their money, laying it pretty thickly on the England side. Of the Hambledon men, Small went in first, and continued until there were about five out, for very few runs, when Nyren went in to him; and then they began to show fight. The mettle of our true blood was roused into full action, and never did they exhibit to finer advantage. Nyren got 98, and Small 110 runs before they were parted. After the former was out the backers came up to Nyren and said, 'You will win the match and we shall lose our money.' The proud old yeoman turned short upon them, and, with that honest independence which gained him the esteem of all parties, told them to their heads that they were rightly served, and that he was glad of it. 'Another time (said he) don't bet your money against such men as we are!' I forget how many runs the Hambledon men got, but, after this turn in affairs, the others stood no chance, and were easily beaten . . .

Upon one occasion, on the Mary-le-bone grounds, I remember Tom Walker going in first, and Lord Frederick Beauclerc giving him the first four balls, all of an excellent length. First four or last four made no difference to Tom—he was always the same cool, collected fellow, Every ball he dropped down just before his bat. Off went his lordship's white hat—dash upon the ground (his constant action when disappointed)—calling him at the same time 'a confounded old beast'.—'I doan't care what ee zays,' said Tom, when one close by asked if he had heard Lord Frederick call him 'an old beast'. No, no; Tom was not the man to be flustered . . .

I cannot do better, in concluding these brief recollections, than enumerate the most eminent players in the Hambledon Club when it was in its glory.

DAVID HARRIS	TOM WALKER
JOHN WELLS	—— ROBINSON
—— PURCHASE	NOAH MANN

WILLIAM BELDHAM   —— SCOTT
JOHN SMALL, JUN.   —— TAYLOR
HARRY WALKER

No eleven in England could have had any chance with these men; and I think they might have beaten any two-and-twenty.

Acknowledgements

The editor and the publishers are indebted to all those who have given permission for the use of material which is their copyright:

Sir Neville Cardus, for 'The Greatest Test Match' and 'Tom Richardson', from *A Cricketer's Book* (Grant Richards), later published as *Days in the Sun* (Jonathan Cape Ltd; later published by Rupert Hart-Davis Ltd)

J. M. Dent & Sons Ltd, for 'Opposing My Hero', from *10 for 66 and All That* by Arthur Mailey

Baskervilles Investments Ltd, for 'The Story of Spedegue's Dropper' from *The Maracot Deep* by Sir Arthur Conan Doyle

Mrs Herbert Farjeon, for 'Herecombe v Therecombe' from *Herbert Farjeon's Cricket Bag* (Macdonald & Co. Ltd) by Herbert Farjeon

Chatto and Windus Ltd, for 'Harold Gimblett', from *Ten Great Innings* by Ralph Barker

Hollis & Carter, for 'Some Memories of the Nineteen-Twenties', from *46 Not Out* by R. C. Robertson-Glasgow

The Marylebone Cricket Club, for the Furniss drawings on page 11